*Food, Conquest, and Colonization
in Sixteenth-Century
Spanish America*

Food, Conquest, and Colonization in Sixteenth-Century Spanish America

John C. Super

University of New Mexico Press

Albuquerque

Library of Congress Cataloging-in-Publication Data

Super, John C., 1944–
    Food, conquest, and colonization in sixteenth-century
Spanish America.

    Bibliography: p.
    Includes index.
    1. Food supply—Latin America—History—16th century.
2. Food crops—Latin America—History—16th century.
3. Diet—Latin America—History—16th century.
4. Indians—Food—History—16th century. I. Title.
HD9014.L32S87   1988   338.1'9'8   87-35767
ISBN 0-8263-1049-4
ISBN 0-8263-1061-3 (pbk.)

Contents

Preface

I became interested in the relationship between food and the early Spanish American past after writing a social and economic history of a province in Mexico. After finishing that work, I began to realize that my efforts to explain social and economic change would have been more successful if placed within the context of the natural world. My working definition of social and economic history had been too narrowly conceived. I then began to look for ways to bridge the gap between the social and the biological worlds, for a way to interpret the relationship between people and environment which might give insight into the processes of conquest and colonization.

Food was the answer for me. As I read Pitirim A. Sorokin's *Hunger as a Factor in Human Affairs*, Redcliffe N. Salaman's *The History and Social Influence of the Potato*, Alfred W. Crosby Jr.'s *The Columbian Exchange*, and the many calorie-counting studies published during the 1960s in the *Annales. E.S.C.*, I became more aware of the complexity of food and more appreciative of its significance for interpreting the past. Food links the social and the natural worlds in marvelously intricate yet encompassing ways. Soil and water, belief and ritual, power and personality, all are a part of the history of food. Food shapes and is shaped by society and nature. It intersects at so many points with the human experience that it can be used to study everything from technology to culture. From this perspective, the history of food simply becomes history.

As with history, the complexity of food leads to its subdivision into component parts, each standing alone to serve the purposes of researchers, but each interconnected in the human experience. The calorie counters, the gastronomes, the nutritionists, the developmentalists, the students of values and beliefs, all have much to say about food in the past and present. My interest in this study is primarily with questions of the availability and distribution of food in sixteenth-century Spanish America. The potential significance of these elementary but difficult questions first occurred to me when writing a brief essay on "The Formation of Nutritional Regimes in Colonial Latin America." In that work I suggested that adequate rather than scarce food supplies might have been the prevailing condition of colonial Latin American nutritional regimes. The present work elaborates on the questions of food availability, and attempts to assess the adequacy of food supplies in the sixteenth century. These are interesting questions in their own right, but I also think that they bear hard on many of the main themes of early Latin American history.

In writing this book, I have relied on research that I have done in the last eight years as I have studied more narrowly defined questions. The American Philosophical Society, the American Council of Learned Societies, the John Carter Brown Library, the National Endowment for the Humanities, and West Virginia University have all at one time or another supported my research on food. I am grateful. Archivists and librarians at the Archivo General de la Nación, the Museo Nacional de Antropología e Historia, the Archivo General de Indias, the John Carter Brown Library, and the inter-library loan librarians at West Virginia University were always helpful.

The organization and principal arguments of the present study have benefitted from the comments of several people. Thomas C. Wright, Woodrow Borah, and Nancy M. Farriss read an early draft and made extensive comments. Peter Bakewell also offered exceptionally good advice on how to rework the book. Gerald Anderson patiently listened to my ideas and helped to clarify them. I also wish to thank David V. Holtby, an editor of the University of New Mexico Press, for the confidence he expressed in an early draft of the book. Finally, thanks to Linda, Jenny, and Andy who continue to help in so many ways.

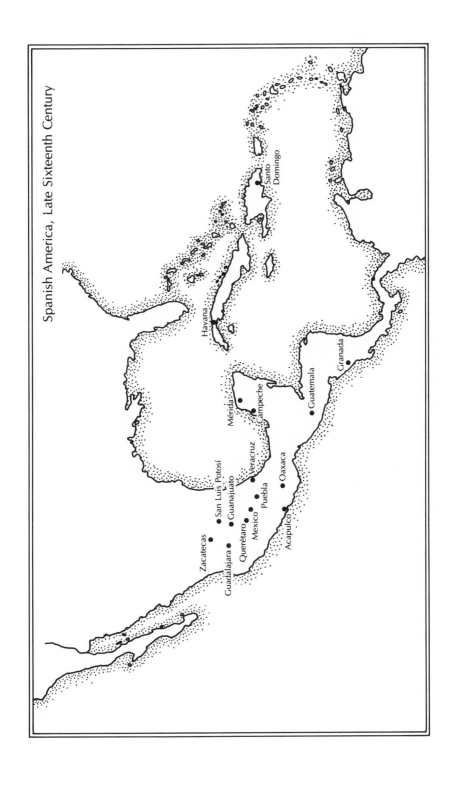

Spanish America, Late Sixteenth Century

Santo Domingo

Granada

Guatemala

Havana

Mérida

Campeche

Veracruz

Zacatecas

San Luis Potosí

Guadalajara

Guanajuato

Querétaro

Mexico

Puebla

Oaxaca

Acapulco

Panamá
Cartagena
Bogotá
Popayán
Quito
Guayaquil
Piura
Trujillo
Lima
Cuzco
Arequipa
La Paz
Potosí
Tucumán
Asunción
Valparaíso
Córdoba
Santiago
Buenos Aires
Concepción

1

Food and History

This book is an inquiry into the relationship between food and history. The setting is sixteenth-century Spanish America, a dynamic and complicated time and place. The principal objective is to come to some understanding of the influence of food on the colonization of the New World.

Food was one of the many material and cultural elements that helped to shape the new social, economic, and political order that emerged in the sixteenth century. Essential to the new order was the ability of natives and colonists to produce, distribute, and consume the foods necessary for survival and growth. The adequacy of food supplies and their impact on early colonization are the main themes of this study. Food supplies were the result of an ever-changing process that embraced the clash of old and new, the struggle to persevere, and the willingness to adjust to the realities of sixteenth-century life. Broad changes in the Atlantic region altered food patterns everywhere. At the local and regional level, the interaction between environment, population, and the economic demands of colonization, buffered by traditional beliefs about food, influenced food supplies. Political structures and decisions were a part of this process. In early Spanish America, local politics usually reflected struggles between competing interest groups whose health and livelihood depended on the outcome of food policies.

Discussing food supplies in a broad chronological and geographical context is difficult. Food is a complex subject, full of nuances and elusive meanings. In societies with diverse cultural and geographic features, generalizations about food are always questionable. In Spanish America, extreme environmental differences influenced food regimes. The contrasts between the fertile temperate regions and the barren highlands were as sharp as those between the range lands and the low coastal zones. Each region supported a particular social and biological system. The systems were influenced and complicated by dozens of practices and institutions—hacienda, mining, tribute, and manufacturing, to name just a few. Further complicating the history of food was the continued existence of multiple production and provisioning systems within the same geographic region. Probably most pervasive was subsistence agriculture, but alongside it were Indian production for markets and the emerging system of European production, which was the most dynamic of the three systems. Each in turn changed as colonial society consolidated and then expanded.

In addition to the diversity and complexity of the subject, and perhaps because of it, there are few extensive analyses of food's influence on historical change in Latin America. Few regions can boast of such detailed studies of food as Louis Stouff's history of provisioning in Provence, John Burnett's analysis of diet in England, or Richard Osborn Cumming's description of food habits in the United States.[1] Much of the current knowledge about food in the Latin American past is a byproduct of research on other subjects or a backward projection of conclusions about food in the twentieth century. No historiographical tradition yet exists outlining the basic principles and dynamics of the many food-related themes in the Latin American past. There are, however, a few interpretations that do seem to represent much of the thinking about food and the past. At the risk of oversimplification, these can be quickly summarized. First, Indian dietary regimes were conservative, selecting and adapting to new foods slowly, if at all. An extension of this position might argue that Indian diets of the sixteenth and twentieth centuries were fundamentally the same.[2] Second, hunger was widespread, increasing with the rise of European domination in the New World. The noted Brazilian historian Caio Prado Júnior wrote that in Pernambuco and Bahia, "there was a chronic dearth of food which frequently amounted to open and widespread famine."[3] Josué de Castro was more dramatic: "All through history, it has been hunger that has hobbled Latin American progress."[4] A corollary to the hypothesis might conclude that the rise of the export economies automatically reduced nutritional levels. With new labor demands and the rise of export prices, the best lands were used for crops destined for the international marketplace, not for workers' diets. Since wages did not keep up with the cost of food, diets declined.[5]

Another idea uses the catastrophic epidemics that lashed Latin America as evidence of inferior diets. Hunger, in other words, helped cause the epidemics. In explaining the colonial population decline, Nicolás Sánchez-Albornoz concluded that "nutritional deficiencies and dietary changes had particularly disastrous results."[6] This is consistent with earlier interpretations of food in English America. Malnutrition, due to the monotony and scarcity of food, weakened populations, making them vulnerable to disease. Beriberi, scurvy, and other nutritional deficiency diseases contributed to the death of colonists.[7]

At times these impressions accurately describe a historical situation. At other times they are based on admittedly scanty evidence, or on projections back in time from problems of hunger today. Most seem consistent, however, with themes of Latin American historiography. Conquest and colonization encouraged poor nutrition as the rise of the Atlantic trading system and the control held by the traditional elites over the exploited masses lessened the food available for consumption.

When I first began to think about food and Latin America, I was convinced that hunger was a widespread condition of the past. It was pervasive, influencing social and economic patterns as much as health. Food as a historical issue could be best understood through a study of scarcity. Consequently, I set out to study the great Mexican famine of 1785–86, agreed on by all as one of the most disastrous times in the history of Mexico. Perhaps the contemporary concern and then the scholarly attention to the famine should have been clues to its proper place in Mexican history. The unprecedented political attention given to the famine was in a curious way an affirmation of the adequacy of food supplies during previous times. Much as the *tumultos* (urban riots) of 1624 and 1692 in Mexico City are in reality much stronger evidence for long-term urban tranquility than for turmoil, the outcry over the famine of 1785–86 is evidence that other times were not nearly as bad.

Others had already recognized this. Sherburne F. Cook and Woodrow Borah have argued that Indian diets actually improved in the aftermath of conquest.[8] Charles Gibson, in explaining the lack of technological progress in agriculture in central Mexico, noted that "the very abundance of the Valley operated to inhibit innovation, for years of poor harvests occurred only intermittently, and no sustained periods of scarcity stimulated experimentation with new methods."[9] Adequate food supplies have not been maintained in the twentieth century. Nevertheless, as Aguirre Beltrán suggests, "the vulgar stereotyping" of Indian diets as the cause of chronic "physical and mental degeneration" is a misrepresentation of Indian life.[10]

The question of what "normal" times were like in the past is receiving increasing attention as historians try to measure food consumption. This is in line with the major direction of applied nutritional research. Nutritionists go into a region today armed with tubes and vials for blood and urine samples, anthropometric tape measures, twenty-four-hour recall forms, and much more. Historians have tried to do the same, using more fragmented evidence and less sophisticated techniques. Since the early work of Earl J. Hamilton on the diet of Spanish sailors, historians have calculated food consumption, telling us that workers in the Levant consumed the equivalent of 1,930 calories a day; agricultural servants in Sweden, 4,315 calories; Polish aristocrats, 4,276–6,092 calories, to mention just a few of the examples available.[11] Overall, in the early modern period, the diet of European peasants consisted of about 2,000 calories a day, almost the same as their Chinese counterparts.[12]

Cook and Borah's conclusions on Indian diets before and after the conquest illustrate some of the difficulties of searching for precision with limited evidence. They calculate that Indian diets increased from 1,400–1,800 calories a day to 1,700–2,200 calories, a range wide enough to account for many different types of production and distribution systems.[13] If their estimates are correct, the Indians of Mexico with their very poor diets still consumed more calories than French peasants on the eve of the revolution, assuming that Le Roy Ladurie's estimate of 1,800 calories a day is correct.[14] Harry Cross's study of nutrition on haciendas in nineteenth-century Mexico states that workers consumed more than 1,600 calories a day in maize alone. Maize, combined with many other foods, including some luxury ones, brought total caloric intakes well above 2,000 calories.[15] Luis Lisanti presents averages as high as 3,416 calories for the São Paulo region in the early nineteenth century, although some communities subsisted on as little as

1,723 calories.[16] Finally, it is worthwhile to mention the "theoretical calcula-tion" of 3,250 calories for sailors and 2,900 calories for soldiers in eigh-teenth-century Chile.[17]

In my study of Spanish sailors' diets in the sixteenth century, I discuss some of the difficulties in trying to quantify consumption. Even though the ration books used to measure diet stated specifically the types and quantities of foods given, it was not possible to prove what and how much sailors ate. Different food preparation and preservation techniques, spoilage and waste, hoarding for sale in the Indies, and falsification of the records made it impossible to arrive at estimates of calories.[18]

The potential of calorie counting for understanding the past has not yet been realized. When protein, vitamins, minerals, and fats become a part of the discussion—as they always should—the problems of sources and methods add new difficulties. Even when historians have faith in their numbers, they at times place too much emphasis on comparisons with recommended daily allowances reported by today's nutritionists. With frag-mentary data from the past and quantity recommendations from the pres-ent, they suggest whether diets were good or bad. René Cravioto warned Mexico about borrowing food composition tables from other countries, mentioning that variations of 500 percent could be found.[19] Historians should heed the warning in applying today's food tables to the past. So far the spatial and chronological limitations of the data prevent any broad statements about the precise quantity of food consumed. Since the data usually come from very narrow institutional sources, comments on the average consumption of calories, protein, vitamins, and minerals have to be phrased cautiously. The pitfalls can be compared to trying to construct a price history when only a score or so of prices scattered through centuries and countries are available.

A second approach to the history of food is through a study of produc-tion. Ultimately this will tell us much about food and the past, although its usefulness for understanding individual consumption patterns is limited. Documentary sources are available that permit the construction of broad profiles of the production of livestock and grains for selected periods. Given a figure for total production, individual consumption is a matter of simple division. The hazards here are readily apparent. In addition to the problems of verifying the statistics, questions about use, distribution, and loss through storage, transportation, and preparation immediately arise. When docu-mentary evidence is not available, another approach, favored by anthropologists, concentrates on the potential productivity of the land. It is possible to have some idea about the carrying capacity of the land, and from this to confirm speculations about population size.[20]

To be done properly, studies of production and consumption have to contend with an interrelated series of problems ranging from chemistry to metrology. The identification of a food item in the diet is only the first step. The conditions of production influence nutrition. More importantly, nutritional values change with age, methods of cooking, techniques of preservation, and use in conjunction with other foodstuffs. A few examples of common sixteenth-century foods illustrate the difficulties. Fresh high-grade beef has 13.6 grams of protein per 100 grams; dried beef, 34.4 grams of protein. Fresh cooked cod has 31 milligrams of calcium per 100 grams; dried, salted cod, 225 milligrams of calcium. Semi-dried *jora* (Andean maize) has 289 calories per 100 grams; dried jora has 340 grams. Maize when eaten alone is deficient in the essential amino acids lysine and tryptophan, but when eaten with pulses the deficiency is less severe. Add to this the problems of calculating basal and other energy needs—correlating energy needs with age, weight, sex, and physical activity—and the difficulties and limitations of consumption studies become apparent.[21] To measure how much was produced and consumed requires settling other problems. Even the basic units of measurement common to a region, such as the *fanega* and *carga* in Mexico, are not yet entirely understood.[22] Very simply, this means conclusions about food values in the past should be viewed as tentative.

Despite the difficulties of analyzing diets, many interesting observations have been made on the relationship between diet and fertility, morbidity, and mortality. How diets influenced population changes remains a basic question. The value of generalizations from research on these problems depends on how well the diet is understood. The complex arguments about synergism (relationship between disease and nutritional state of host), for example, have questionable value for historical interpretations if the quantity and quality of the diet cannot be precisely determined.[23]

A third approach is to use wage and price data to illustrate consumption trends. This approach does not overcome the many problems of nutritional analysis, but it does help to verify the consumption and production data. Borah and Cook initiated the discussion in 1958, but little has been done since then.[24] There are some complete accounts of prices during the long term, but without comparable wage data it is hard to generalize about production and distribution.[25] Once wage and price series are available for different regions and times, the potential of a given group for an adequate diet can be specifically stated. This will be helpful, but attempts to prove the content of diet will confront the same obstacles faced by the ration studies.

These different approaches are in one way or another interested in measuring food supply. This remains central to analyzing the many complex, not yet entirely understood, ways in which nutrition affects population, intelligence, perceptions, and behavior. Many hypotheses about food and the past are based on assumptions about the quantity and quality of the diet. Yet one of the few conclusions that can be drawn from the historical literature is that the evidence has not yet yielded the precise data necessary to support the hypotheses.

This is expected in a new area of inquiry, where scholars are still experimenting with sources and methods. Much of the work has been of a pioneering nature, laying the foundation for thinking about food in the past. In the chapters that follow the influence of this work is often seen. What is not seen, however, is an estimate of the calories consumed by different groups. As I see it, the study of food in the past is too influenced by the recent study of nutrition, with its attention to measuring nutrients. For sixteenth-century Spanish America the sources and methods are not yet available to answer the question of how much and how well people ate in the same way that nutritionists would try to answer the question for today's populations.

While it is hard to talk about individual diets, it is possible to discuss food supplies in general by evaluating those biological and social forces that influenced what and how much people ate.[26] It is even possible to arrive at some assessment of the adequacy of the diet, much as it is possible to arrive at an understanding of the size of a galaxy without counting all of its stars. Traditional sources and methods can carry us a long way toward understanding the nature of the food supply system. They point to the major foods, their geographic and social distribution, and the way in which political institutions affected food availability. They also reveal much about change in the nutritional regimes of sixteenth-century people. Irrefutable proof of the quantity of food produced and consumed will be lacking, but a sense of the adequacy of the diet can be presented.

Adequate is difficult to define, since its precise meaning is relative to time and place. It is as much a state of mind, a perception that influences the way people think about life, as an actual condition of availability. By *adequate*, I mean a supply of food that usually meets the nutritional and cultural needs of consumers, and that is distributed widely enough to prevent large pockets of continuous hunger in any region or social group. For example, for those dependent on a market economy, an adequate food supply means there is sufficient food in relation to other goods of value to keep the price of food low enough for those groups with small incomes to feed their families.

Ideally, to answer the question of how well people ate the focus should be on the distribution and actual consumption of foods, not on their availability. Generous food supplies do not mean that all ate well, nor do food shortages mean that all ate poorly. At times there is enough evidence to assume that abundant foods led to full stomachs, at other times there is not. Without the evidence, it is necessary to talk about food in a more general way. This limits the use of hypotheses in the more complex arguments about nutrition and demography, but it does open the way for viewing food from different vantage points.

Food was more than nutrients, and its influence in the past went far beyond dietary patterns. After language, food in many ways was the most fundamental expression of shared human activity in early Spanish America. Its trail can be followed in many different directions, connecting people to land, city to countryside, colony to metropolis, belief to behavior. As expected, the trail is not always well marked, and at times it seems to double back. Conclusions depend on what is emphasized and the problems under investigation. The contradictory, inconsistent nature of the evidence presents special problems.

Take for example contemporary observations on Mexico in the 1550s. An Englishman noted of Mexico City that "beefe, mutton, and hennes, capons, quailes, and Guiny-cockes, and such like, all are very good cheape [*sic*]."[27] Alonso de Zorita writes of Indian workers during the same period who "are made to toil from dawn to dusk, in the raw cold of morning and afternoon, in wind and storm, without other food than those rotten or dried out tortillas, and even of this they have not enough."[28] By contrast, a few years earlier, a government official wrote that the Indians of Oaxaca "live without necessity if they want to work because they are so well supplied with bread, fruit, gold, cotton, and cacao."[29] In 1556, a politician in Puebla complained that "for New Spain it is always a year of famine," occasioned by poor policy and the flight of Indian workers to the cacao fields of the south where they become rich.[30] Two years later in the same city a Spaniard complained that he had 300 bushels of wheat, but "couldn't find anyone to offer me a penny for it in the valley."[31]

What to make of such diversity? Analysis of the evidence can find weaknesses: the overzealous administrator, the naive foreigner, the lonely

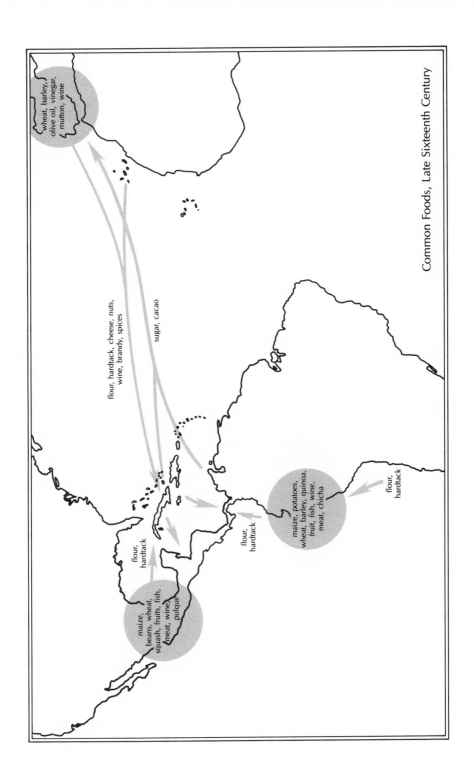

wheat, barley, olive oil, vinegar, mutton, wine

flour, hardtack, cheese, nuts, wine, brandy, spices

sugar, cacao

maize, potatoes, wheat, barley, quinoa, fruit, fish, wine, meat, chicha

flour, hardtack

flour, hardtack

flour, hardtack

maize, beans, wheat, squash, fruits, fish, meat, wine, pulque

Common Foods, Late Sixteenth Century

immigrant, all distorting what they saw. The same applies to the chroniclers, those always-suspect observers of the early days of colonization. The chroniclers are particularly interesting because they were concerned with hot and cold, good and bad, abundance and scarcity. They express opinions while giving descriptions. Consequently, they have to be used with care. Charles Boxer summarized the difficulty when he contrasted their emphasis on beauty, fertility, and abundance in Brazil with the reality of drought, bad soil, and insects.[32] Chroniclers lied, or at best distorted reality. This is a fair assessment of some chroniclers, but it does not hold up as a general indictment of the chroniclers as sources for the material history of the New World. Many chroniclers wrote with a balanced hand, giving accurate descriptions of the good and the bad.

More problematic is the risk in generalizing from the few sources available. Patterns of the production and consumption of food depended on many influences that intersected, overlapped, and changed through time. These are mentioned in the following pages, but they should be emphasized at the outset. Urban and rural diets might differ, but not according to any fixed principle. Independent rural proprietors or members of small communities had the advantage of hunting and gathering to supplement agriculture. Dependent rural workers often had fixed rations as part of a wage schedule, with the advantage that these were given even during times of scarcity. Urban people did not have access to as rich an environment, but they did have diversity, credit systems, and a political organization that sought to maintain an adequate supply of food.

Temperate and tropical climates helped to distinguish diets and food availability. Today the fragility of tropical environments is widely appreciated. In the past, when population pressure and commercial crop demands were less imposing, tropical environments supplied abundant carbohydrates, minerals, and vitamins. They were less capable, however, of offering protein than were the temperate regions, with their grain and livestock resources. Income and participation in some type of social service network were also crucial in determining diet. So were marketing and transportation systems. Beliefs about food and manners of preparation and consumption played a part too in influencing what people ate.

In addition to these more or less continuous patterns influencing supplies and consumption, there were short-term interruptions that limited diet. Weather shifts, disease, warfare, transport delays, and the opening up of new mining territories reduced the availability of food. Together, these qualifications might suggest that Frédéric Mauro's description of Europe is appropriate for Spanish America: "What is most striking is the irregularity of diets according to season, time, social class, environment, circumstance."[33]

This would be a judicious conclusion. Perhaps it would even be possible to work out a scheme estimating the nutrients consumed by different groups, although the estimates would always be open to criticism. All would be helpful, but not entirely satisfying. Much as demographic history should move beyond numbers to discuss cause, effect, and significance, nutritional history should move beyond a description of diet to discuss food as a general historical problem, significant for efforts of interpretation and synthesis.

In selecting the evidence to discuss the Spanish American experience, I have concentrated on Mexico and the central Andes, the centers of Indian and European life in the sixteenth century. Evidence that seems to reflect basic conditions and perceptions of food over the long term receives the most attention. The intent has been to concentrate on evidence that reveals plausible, usually coherent, and intelligible patterns of food and change. Simple attempts to tally the number of times contemporaries spoke of plenty or scarcity would not lead very far. In some cases I might err in pushing the evidence too far, but I hope that the discussion in the text is sufficient to point out the tentative nature of some of the arguments. In many ways, the following chapters should be considered as an exploratory essay, probing the dimensions of the question of food supply, evaluating some of the evidence, and looking at the relationship between food and selected characteristics of social, political, and economic life. The result is a series of observations and hypotheses about food in sixteenth-century Spanish America.

2

Land and Food

Little in the background of conquerors and colonizers prepared them for the immensity of the New World—the endless stretches of tropical lowlands, the vast semi-arid plains, and the spacious, fertile valleys. The size and openness of the land lured Europeans forward, challenging them first to explore and then to settle.

Space for crops and animals from the New and Old Worlds was readily available. The conquest actually increased the availability of land because the intensively cultivated farms and gardens that had supported large Indian populations lay fallow or reverted to a wild state. The dynamics of colonization created emptiness where there had once been much activity. By the 1570s, when Spaniards had firmly established themselves, López de Velasco could note that "the land was uncultivated almost everywhere."[1] Viceroys reported that land was an unlikely source of revenue because there "was much more than Spaniards needed."[2] This generalization ignored the active market that had developed in some rural areas by the end of the century, but it did reveal a basic condition of early colonization. Ample land was available for subsistence and commercial agriculture. As the seventeenth century progressed, a stillness surrounded once-busy fields.[3] Compared to Spain, where about one-half the land was sown in the seventeenth century, Latin America was uncultivated, empty and waiting for new agricultural enterprises.[4] The same was true in the mid-twentieth century, when only 12 to 18 percent of tropical Latin America was cultivated.[5]

Conquest and colonization repopulated the land at the same time that they depopulated it. In less than fifty years, Spaniards had explored much of the new land, destroying and creating as they advanced. Within another fifty years, they had established communities stretching from northern Mexico to southern Chile, remaking the land to suit their purposes. Despite the challenges and uncertainties of cultivation, the land was generous, yielding enough to satisfy the nutritional needs of conquest and colonization. Technical and managerial skills helped, but more basic was the ease with which European plants and animals adjusted to different soil and climatic conditions. Out of the mixing of Indian and European cultures, new nutritional regimes emerged, which were more satisfying than those that had existed before the conquest. The diversity of the climatic zones and the fertility of the soils helped create the regimes, guaranteeing the foods necessary for colonization. Even the prairies and semi-arid lands, although resistant to hoe and plow, played their part by supporting sheep and cattle in numbers unheard of in Europe.

Impressions of Productivity

The abundance and fertility of the land were consistent with beliefs about the abundance of foods. Enthusiastic writers described the delicious and soothing fruits, ripe for the picking, that nourished many a settler during the early days of conquest. Some areas were so fertile that "even if walking lost, [you] will not die of hunger."[6] Such views probably overstate the availability of natural foods, although it is well to keep in mind that tropical fruits continue to serve as subsistence foods in the diet of the Latin American poor today.[7] Equally exciting to Europeans was the abundance of game and fowl. Dozens of varieties of small game—some of which had been introduced by Europeans—hid in small thickets and ran through plains and forests. Deer and rabbits were so plentiful near Quito in the 1570s that a "soldier with a harquebus could take six or seven deer at night, and it seems that the supply is inexhaustible." In the valleys south of Quito, "twenty boys from the Indian parish with their sticks could catch three hundred rabbits by midday."[8] Outside Mexico City, extensive lakes and abundant natural vegetation supported much fish and game. Indians used blow guns to bring down waterfowl, bows and arrows to fell deer, nets to trap hares, spears and lines to catch fish.[9] Toward the end of the eighteenth century, after two hundred fifty years of environmental change and the destruction of feeding grounds, Mexico City residents still trapped and ate enough fowl during the annual migrations to offset shortages in meat markets. In the provinces game was more abundant.[10]

For men and women from temperate latitudes, agriculture in the tropics was more remarkable than the abundance of game. In the lower and intermediate elevations, the lack of frosts plus good rains ensured adequate supplies of maize and cassava. Some trees even yielded fruit all year. What a marvel to have delicious fruits and melons in the middle of winter, exclaimed many visitors to the tropical zones. Foods ripened so quickly and grew so large that even the usually cautious and analytical observer could be caught up in the enthusiasm for New World agriculture.[11]

Spain contributed its share of foods to the new nutritional regimes.[12] Wheat, rice, and barley headed the list of grains. From the earliest voyages, Spaniards had also brought fruits and vegetables almost too numerous to mention: radishes, asparagus, brussels sprouts, beets, spinach, oranges, limes, peaches, pears, apricots, figs, quinces, melons, cherries, grapes, sugar cane, and more. By 1526 the price of carrots, cauliflower, beans, turnips, horseradish, and lettuce was already falling in Mexico City markets.[13] Spices were not ignored in the food trade, and even provincial towns had their cloves, cinnamon, and the all-important saffron.[14]

Of the plant foods introduced, bananas and plantains probably had the most far-reaching consequences for diet. They quickly grew in importance until they had achieved the status of a staple in the tropical zones, admired for their ease of cultivation, and their delicate, sustaining flavor. Comparable to maize, wheat, and rice in other areas, they were used to make everything from breads to drinks.[15] This does not exhaust the list of plant foods. Africa sent directly millet, sorghum, squash, horsebeans, and ginger, but their sixteenth-century influence is not easy to trace in Spanish America. In Brazil, even the potentially useful millet had the reputation of being better for livestock than humans.[16]

Animal foods surpassed many of the plant foods in nutritional value. Cattle, sheep, and goats accompanied Spaniards on the early expeditions, adding abundant new sources of protein. Cattle did not survive in the high elevations, nor sheep in the tropical lowlands, but everywhere else they became a part of Indian diets. So did pigs and chickens, which now joined turkeys and guinea pigs as parts of Indian estates.

Quito, more than any other region, symbolized the productivity of the new nutritional regimes. From the early comments of Cieza de León in the 1540s to the eighteenth-century descriptions of Clavijero, Quito was a land "where the delights of the country are enjoyed all the year, and the earth is continually adorned with herbs and flowers."[17] Lima lacked the agricultural hinterland of Quito, but it too enjoyed well-supplied markets of fresh fruits and vegetables throughout the year. Traveling from place to place in Peru, Bernabé Cobo saw the same crops at different stages of growth, which explained the continual supply of foods.[18] Visitors from Europe "passed the most comfortable, pleasant, and delectable Lent that could be imagined because of the convenience of the many fruits and greens that come in that period of penitence."[19] Markets in Mexico City had the same abundance of American and European foods.[20] Clavijero expressed it most succinctly: "In Europe there is but one feed time, and one harvest. In New Spain there are several."[21]

A longer growing season and climatic differences within short distances distinguished tropical nutritional regimes from those in Europe. Before the advent of canning and the transportation revolution in the nineteenth century, diets in the temperate latitudes depended on the season. Compared to tropical Latin America, the European and temperate American food cycle followed a rigid schedule of planting and harvesting. Greens and vegetables were available during the summer, but began to perish by fall. Apples were one of the few fruits that kept into winter. Fresh meat was only a memory after fall butchering. Families were left facing the long winter with dried pork, beans, turnips, and a longing for spring.[22]

By contrast, in much of tropical Spanish America the climatic differences within short distances encouraged year-round planting and harvesting of some crops. This contributed to an active interregional trade in food. For example, in Peru the food trade linked the highland plateaus, temperate basins, tropical lowlands, and coastal plains. Potatoes, quinoa, wheat, maize, beans, sugar, honey, bananas, fish, beef, pork, and scores of other foods strained the backs of llamas as they found their way back and forth between hot and cold lands.[23]

Space was both an advantage and a disadvantage. Land was available for cultivating food, but distance was always an obstacle to its transport. Spaniards, despite their familiarity with other parts of the Indies, were still unprepared for the rigors of travel in the Andes Mountains. One witness described the road from Lima to Cuzco, the two principal cities of the realm, as "the worst road I have ever traveled, and it seems that it is one of the worst, most rugged in the world."[24] Baffled by the region's deserts, tropical valleys, and towering peaks, early arrivals—like those who followed— reduced the Andes to zones in their effort to comprehend the region's complexity and vastness.[25]

The Andes, striking in their grandeur and many moods, both repulsed and attracted settlers. Eventually Spaniards controlled a string of permanent settlements that extended from Bogotá in the north to the cool and windy city of Potosí in the south. The basin of Quito supported the largest northern settlement, influencing developments to the north and south. Ibarra and Tulcán were microcosms of Quito, much more stable than the small valleys of Loja and Zaruma that experienced flashes of growth due to the discovery of gold. In the south the basins turn into broader, flatter surfaces. The densely populated valleys of Cajamarca, Huancayo, almost as large as the valley of Mexico, and Cuzco produced substantial quantities of grains and tubers. Mountain barriers separated these high valleys from the lower ones, where the productivity of fruits and vegetables matched that of highland grains and tubers.

Coastal valleys were almost as isolated as the mountainous ones. Along most of the coast, Spaniards encountered the *llanos*, or desert coastal plains, that extended from Túmbez in the north to Arequipa in the south. In this land of shifting sands and rocky hills, even scrappy desert plants have a hard time surviving. The great *arenales*, mounds of moving sand that made travel difficult, most impressed intruders.[26] The barren fastness was interrupted by river oases, which became much-sought-after refuges. Early civilizations had built cities along the river valleys of Piura, Chiclayo, Pativiles, and Ica. Spaniards did the same, taking advantage of the rich alluvial soils, re-plenished as the mountain-fed rivers sought the sea. Pizarro decided to build the new city of Lima next to one of the rivers.

Less serious geographic obstacles faced settlers in Mexico. The Valley of Mexico, stretching fifty miles north to south and thirty miles east to west was the nutritional center of the colony, as it had been of the Aztec empire. Within two decades after conquest, a hundred mule trains carried fruits, grains, and imported foods and drink to Mexico city. In the early seventeenth century, it is said that a thousand canoes brought in goods daily.[27] Just to the west of the Valley of Mexico, the Valley of Toluca, perched at 8,000 feet above sea level, produced grains and livestock. In the southwest, the Valley of Morelos had become an important food and sugar center by 1600. To the south, the broad, fertile plain of Puebla yielded surplus grains for Mexico City and the Caribbean. To the north, the expansive basin of Guanajuato, known as the Bajío, supported maize and wheat farms and cattle and sheep ranches. As the sixteenth century drew to a close, some of the satellite basins rivalled that of Mexico in agricultural wealth.[28]

Smaller basins to the south, hidden away between great volcanic uplifts, had good soils and supported dense Indian populations, but their smaller level surfaces limited production, at least in comparison to the central valleys. North of the central region, the highland plateaus and basins seldom offered the agricultural advantages of the center. The main route of exploration and colonization was between the Sierra Madre Oriental and Sierra Madre Occidental, a plateau that lost elevation and moisture as it spread north. More than anything else, the uncertain rains limited agriculture in the north. With adequate rains, range grasses supported herds and flocks, and farms produced grains and vegetables.

On the Pacific slope of the Sierra, settlers built towns along the rivers that flowed down from the mountain snow packs. Most were small and lacked foods and amenities that Spaniards considered essential for life. The northeastern Gulf coastal plain, wider and more fertile than the Pacific coastal plain, did not attract as many settlers in the sixteenth century. Most settlement was to the south of Tampico. In what is now the states of Veracruz and Tabasco, permanent towns took hold, nourished by adequate rains and good maize harvests. Rainfall lessened as the Yucatan peninsula swung north, making agriculture a risky enterprise. Not risky enough, though, to hamper the growth of Campeche, Mérida, and Valladolid.

The New World easily accommodated the new arrivals. Land pressure was seldom extreme enough to limit the foods necessary for survival and growth. Geography, however, did influence the types of food available. Communities at a climatic disadvantage or on the periphery of regular trade routes had restricted diets. Spaniards in Culiacán supposedly lived on fish and maize tortillas.[29] Cartagena relied on Magdalena River traffic for its supplies of wheat, barley, and hams. Without the traffic, cassava and maize became staples. Yet it had enough of these—and of cattle—to make Spanish naval officers consider it a very suitable port.[30] Guayaquil had tropical fruits and much fish and game, but depended on the highlands for its grain.[31]

Cities that served the aims of empire relied on a wider trading network than did the small provincial towns. The political decisions of empire builders contributed to the nutritional success of these cities. Panama was a vital city in the Spanish scheme of empire, linking the west coast of South America to the Caribbean and Spain. Inadequate Indian food supplies forced early colonists to eat shellfish for survival. Local fruits, supplemented by citrus, figs, and plantains helped, but by the 1570s local agriculture was still not sufficient for the needs of four hundred Spanish households. Much food had to be imported. It came overland, hauled on the backs of mules, or pulled in barges up the Chagres River. By the end of the century, increasingly large amounts of food—wine and brandy from Peru, wheat and hardtack from Ecuador—came by ship.[32] Nombre de Dios on the other side of the isthmus was even more dependent on trade. According to testimony from 1561, "It is publicly and widely known that if Spain, the islands, or Peru do not supply maize, chickens, wheat, cassava and other foods this land suffers great want."[33] Interruptions in these supplies forced reliance on local fruits and livestock, but there is little evidence of widespread and continuing hunger.

The same was true in the Caribbean islands. Although climate hampered the growth of temperate crops, Spain stubbornly encouraged wheat cultivation.[34] The hopes for wheat did not materialize, leaving the islands to pigs, cattle, maize, and cassava. All produced so abundantly that the islands continued to hold a deserved reputation as a source of food supplies in the late sixteenth century, long after the disappointment caused by exhausted mineral wealth. Loss of population and a decline in gold production—not a shortage of food—hampered the islands.[35] Only sugar cane, ideally suited to the red Matanzas clay and tropical climate, had the potential to rescue the islands from economic somnambulism. The "abundant meat, cassava, and maize" of the 1580s eased the transition to plantation agriculture.[36]

Potosí was more of a challenge to provision. Like a powerful potentate, Potosí sat on the throne of the richest silver mine in the world, drawing food resources from an expanding kingdom. In the 1570s, the most pessimistic observers said that nothing grew around the city, not even a blade of grass. Fires to heat the giant smelting caldrons had consumed all the available trees. Pack trains strung along the narrow trails supplied most of the food. Dried fish from Arica and Atacama; frozen fish from Collao; nuts, rice, and herbs from Chile; potatoes and barley from the high plateaus; maize and fruits from the valleys; acrid maté tea from Paraguay; all and more kept the city alive.[37] The provisioning network was staggering in its size and complexity. When it broke down, whether due to administrative ineptitude or changes in the weather, shortages ensued. Yet people kept coming to Potosí, some excited by the silver, others caught in an increasingly demanding labor system. By 1611, according to one observer, the provisioning system had to support close to 150,000 people.[38] Even if the population was half that size, the survival of the city was a credit to the organizational abilities of Indians and Spaniards, and to a productive hinterland.

In addition to supplying mining and port cities, sixteenth-century agriculture had to meet the substantial food needs of the military. Reports from military planners in Spain often proclaimed the abundance of the Indies. By the 1570s, and probably long before, ships sailing from Spain depended on finding meats, grains, and tubers in the Indies for the return voyage.[39] In the 1580s, central Mexico was shipping hardtack, flour, garbanzos, meat, fish, oil, and vinegar to Havana. Agriculturally rich regions in Peru supplied similar foods for soldiers heading to the Indian campaigns in Chile. Belief in the abundance of provisions cannot be dismissed as uninformed judgments made in Spain. Rations for soldiers in Mexico in the 1580s called for two pounds of meat or one pound of salted fish a day, compared to one pound of meat or one-third pound of salted fish a day for those provisioned in Spain.[40]

Contemporaries described a rich, varied world of foods, usually sufficient in quality and quantity to meet basic local needs, and usually with enough surplus to supply dependent cities. Not all observers were as ebullient as Vázquez de Espinosa, who saw every valley as fertile, every plain crowded with livestock, every town stuffed with provisions, but few offered evidence of severe, widespread shortages. Instead, they appreciated the unique advantages of climate, crop diversity, and longer growing season that tropical Latin America enjoyed over temperate Europe.[41]

Crop Yields

Contemporary impressions of productivity are not easy to cross-validate. Statements of seed-yield ratios are one of the very few ways that contemporaries tried to generalize about agricultural productivity. The ratios are imperfect measures at best, but they do provide one basis for interpreting the productivity of agriculture. Yields of one thousand to one for maize and four hundred to one for wheat were occasionally reported, but they exaggerate the general productivity of grains.[42] Yields varied quite sharply from region to region and crop to crop, seldom exceeding one hundred to one for the primary grains. Poor soils, as in Abancay high in the Andes, held the yields of wheat, maize, and barley to eight or nine *fanegas* for each one sown. In Piura, along the coast, the major grains did much better, yielding from forty to eighty *fanegas* for one. Around Quito, perhaps the major center of Andean grain production, wheat gave from ten to twenty for one, and maize from twenty to fifty for one. Loja had even a better record, producing thirty to one hundred for one of maize, and thirty to fifty for one of wheat.[43] In Ycatlan, New Galicia, wheat yielded sixty for one, and maize two hundred for one. A little to the south, in Guadalajara, wheat produced ten to twenty for one; farther south still, in Puebla, the best agricultural lands of Mexico, wheat gave one hundred for one.[44]

This patchwork of numbers is interesting, but has its limits as a method of analyzing early agriculture. The harvesting of a crop was the culmination of human effort and commitment balanced against soil and climate. Land, water, labor, fertilizer, and transportation all influenced agriculture, which makes generalizations about yields suspect. The highest yields came from fertilized and irrigated lands. The use of guano and fish as fertilizers boosted the yields of the already productive soils of the coastal river basins. In the wheat plains north of Mexico City, irrigation increased yields and also provided insurance against droughts.[45] Total real costs for these and other sixteenth-century agricultural investments are difficult to calculate. One impression is that the costs were lower than in Europe, where pressure on the land increased rather than decreased in the sixteenth century. Although the real costs of production remain elusive, comparisons with Europe suggest the advantages of New World agriculture.

European grain yields during the Middle Ages were slight, seldom exceeding three for one. When yields were that low, disaster followed bad years as farmers ate grain needed for next year's planting. Technological and field-use innovations in the fourteenth and fifteenth centuries increased production, but yields of major grains still averaged less than six for one in the sixteenth century.[46] In Spain, matters were worse. "A year which yielded four times the amount sown was considered to be abundant; very good if it gave five times; extraordinary if six to seven times were harvested."[47] What was extraordinary in Spain was ordinary in Spanish America.

Little wonder that yields of the new lands astonished observers. Garcilaso de la Vega, one of the best storytellers of the sixteenth century, recounted what a Peruvian wheat farmer had told him in 1560. "Eat some of this bread, for it is part of a yield of more than three hundred for one. That will give you something to tell in Spain."[48] Some eighteenth-century writers continued to emphasize crop productivity. Humboldt exclaimed that "The fecundity of *tlaolli*, or Mexican maize, is so much that it could not be imagined in Europe." His analysis of wheat reached the same conclusion.

While grain production in France averaged five to six for one, Mexico produced seventeen to twenty-four, Buenos Aires sixteen, Montevideo twelve, and Cajamarca eighteen to twenty for one. On average, American lands yielded two to three times as much as European lands.[49]

Recent analyses of yield do not always agree. Tribute harvests from small towns around Lake Texcoco in the sixteenth century dropped to a ridiculously low twenty-five *fanegas* harvested for ten sown. Measured in yield per hectare, averages were 67 to 72 kilograms per hectare. The best lands usually gave far less than fifty for one, seldom reaching 500 kilograms per hectare.[50] These were very low yields for maize, inconsistent with most contemporary observations. Perhaps production ratios were so low because Indians simply did not plant as much seed in as much land as they were supposed to have done. Certainly other data suggest much higher production, reaching an average of 1,060 kilograms per hectare during the first years of colonization.[51]

Studies of eighteenth-century Mexican wheat agriculture also question the assumption of high yields. Eric Van Young states that irrigated production in the Guadalajara region was comparable to unirrigated production in Europe. That would make the eight to ten for one yield of the Guadalajara region unimpressive.[52] David Brading in his study of León also emphasizes low yields. "If measured by the acreage planted [yield] was quite low, and indeed, was more reminiscent of medieval Europe than the 'age of improvement.' " Brading then mentions higher estimates that were "certainly equal, but hardly superior, to the best English returns of that period."[53]

The question of grain yields is not resolved for the sixteenth or eighteenth century. My opinion is that the claims of sixteenth-century observers will be upheld by further research. Specific productivity ratios depended on many influences, but yields were generally higher than in Europe. Two underlying reasons for the higher yields were the reversion of tilled land to fallow after the decline of the Indian population, and the vast expanse of virgin lands on the peripheries of settlements. Low man-land ratios freed America from many of the dilemmas facing Europe.

Multiple harvests of the same crop sharpened the differences with Europe. By the 1540s, the intensively worked land of the Peruvian river valleys supposedly produced two crops of maize a year.[54] Two and even three maize crops a year in Mexico were reported, but this was not a general condition.[55] Belief in multiple crop yields probably overestimated the richness of agriculture, though such an authority as Carl Sauer noted that four crops a year could be grown in the tropics.[56]

Tubers were as important to food supply as grains, their availability throughout the year just as impressive to Europeans. The yield of tubers such as potatoes and cassava is widely appreciated today, but unlike the many references to maize and wheat there were few early estimates of yield. The earliest I have seen is from the 1640s, when Du Tertre mentioned that land planted in cassava fed six times as many as the best French lands planted in wheat.[57] In addition to yielding more than wheat and maize, the tubers were hardier, more resistant to changes in the weather, less vulnerable to droughts and pests, and could be harvested at different times of the year.[58]

Bananas and plantains, first planted in the Caribbean in 1516, then carried to the mainland in the 1520s, outproduced even the tubers. Within a generation, they had spread through much of tropical America, emerging as a staple for the poorer classes, who used them in combination with tubers and grains. Bananas enjoyed such popularity because they consistently outproduced traditional staples, required little work, only some weeding now and then, and produced throughout the year. Nutritionally, bananas supplied abundant carbohydrates, vitamins, and minerals. Humboldt was astounded at the productivity of bananas, calculating that they produced one hundred thirty-three times more food by weight than wheat and forty-four more than potatoes.[59] In calories produced per unit of land, bananas led all of the common staples of the sixteenth century. Then came manioc and potatoes, followed by maize, wheat, barley, and rice.[60] Translated into the practical necessities of life, this meant that five days of work produced enough bananas for one year.[61]

Inhabitants of Spanish America experienced nutritional regimes very different from those in Europe. The combination of European and American foods created diversified, nutritionally rich diets. Crop yields were higher than those in Europe, and longer or staggered growing seasons made fresh food available during much of the year. The potential for one of the best diets in the history of the world was evident soon after discovery of the New World. For Europeans, the introduction of livestock and wheat was an essential step in creating that diet.

3

Meat and Bread

After a diet of hardtack and salted meat, the standard fare of the Atlantic crossing, Spanish sailors and colonists longed for fresh foods. On arrival in the New World, they found an abundance of fresh fruits and vegetables. The same was not true for meats and breads. Few Spaniards thought desirable the edible *hutía* and *corie* (animals that resembled rodents and hares) that ran through the fields and forests of the islands, nor did they favor the abundant iguana, even though its meat was "as good as or better than that of rabbits."[1] In central Mexico, only the very hungry and indiscriminate Spaniards ate dogs and the many wild things in and around the lakes. In the Andes, the cameloids, llama, vicuña, and especially the small *pacos* were good sources of protein during times of emergency, but none had lasting appeal. Other animals, such as *bizcachas* and *cuyes* (similar to hares and guinea pigs), were important foods in Indian households but seldom became a regular feature of European diets. Indian breads also had their limitations. Breads made from cassava and maize satisfied early nutritional needs, evoking praise from a few chroniclers. For most Spaniards, however, they did not deliver the same gustatory satisfaction as wheat bread. Other grains, such as amaranth and quinoa, were eaten by Spaniards, but remained typically Indian foods.

Preference for European meats and grains unleashed powerful forces that affected sixteenth-century life. Finding native staples unsatisfactory, Spaniards introduced their own foods, which challenged Indian staples for dominance of the land. The struggle between European and Indian foods was part of the broader drama of the conquest and colonization of America. The results were complex, as diets were modified and changed through time. Eventually a balance was reached, one that provided all the nutrients necessary for rapid colonization by Spain without displacing the staples of Indian diets.

Livestock

Old World livestock raced across the islands and mainland, adapting to their new environment and creating new nutritional and social relationships. From the Caribbean to the central region of Mexico and the highlands of Peru, European quadrupeds found favorable pastures and a benign climate. Without serious competition for the natural pastures, livestock quickly spread to the edges of the semi-arid zones. Observers witnessed a phenomenon new to them and were duly impressed. Even before 1500 reports noted "infinite numbers of livestock" and "many chickens" in Hispaniola.[2] The abundance of meat was all the more noteworthy because of the shortages in Europe.[3]

Wherever Spaniards went, they took their livestock with them. Pigs, sheep, and cattle were as much a part of the conquest as Toledo steel and fighting mastiffs. Even if the explorers did not remain, the stock did, adjusting to the new environment and surviving the attacks of predators. Later expeditions were often surprised to find large herds of animals, the only traces of forgotten earlier attempts at colonization.[4]

In Spain, both pocketbook and stomach profited most from sheep, animals closely associated with Spanish history since the Middle Ages. In Spanish America, first pigs and then cattle were dominant. The growing demand for hides, for fat to substitute for olive oil, and for tallow for lubricants and candles guaranteed the eventual primacy of cattle. In addition, cattle hides supplied an international market, while American wool never competed with Spanish wool. Sheep experienced real difficulty living in the lowland tropics, but since Spaniards did too, they seldom had to worry about shortages of mutton.[5]

From maybe 1,000 cattle introduced by Spain, vast herds of *criollo* cattle soon grazed the seemingly endless pasture.[6] Within one generation after discovery, livestock threatened to overrun some of the Caribbean islands. Unprecedented quantities of meat and hides became available. The casual slaughter of so many animals worried a few forward-looking administrators, especially since animals were used just for hides and fat, but real shortages did not develop until much later.[7] By the 1520s, there were so many cattle on Hispaniola that officials petitioned for the establishment of a *mesta* (livestock guild) to control the herds.[8] Wild dogs reportedly killed 60,000 cows a year in the 1560s, but this barely affected the size of the herds.[9] In the early seventeenth century, some of the islands still produced more than 10,000 *arrobas* of "excellent lard and many poor people benefit from it."[10] The surplus protein was especially important for the maintenance of the fleets moving back and forth across the Atlantic. Pigs on the hoof were about as important as salted and smoked beef. Fed with maize stored on board, pigs provided fresh meat for the return voyage.[11]

Central Mexico, particularly the basins to the north and west of Mexico City, soon surpassed the Caribbean as a producer of protein. Already by the end of the 1520s, meat and pork prices had begun to fall in the markets of Mexico City. Pigs were so numerous that the *cabildo* (city council) had to busy itself devising ways to keep them of the streets.[12] The rapid drop in prices assured the city of an adequate supply of protein by the early 1530s.[13] Expansion outward from the central valley continued the remarkable growth. Herds and flocks of twenty and even forty thousand soon grazed on the grassy plains north of the central valley. Vast tracts of land were awarded to the new cattle kings, but most of the growth took place on open common lands. There were so many cattle that many were left unbranded.[14] Lesley Byrd Simpson estimated the number of cattle at 800,000 and the number of sheep and goats at 4.6 million in 1600.[15] The northern movement of livestock lessened supplies available for Mexico City, but observers still mentioned that cattle were killed just for their hides in the 1590s.[16]

The Andean valleys also supported large populations of sheep and cattle. By the end of the sixteenth century, meat had identifiable characteristics, depending on whether it came from the highlands or lowlands. The basins around Quito, where grasses known as *quijones* gave the meat a delicate flavor, were the best-known cattle regions. Cattle shipments from Quito supplied towns to the north and south.[17] Around Lima livestock caused so much damage to maize and cassava lands that special laws, and eventually special corrals, were needed to contain them.[18] Altitude and competition with Andean cameloids restrained the growth of cattle in the highlands, but did not stop them from contributing to the new nutritional regimes.[19]

The geographic configuration of livestock raising changed constantly, helping to direct the process of colonization. The effective settlement of Spanish America came on the heels of range cattle that were driven farther and farther away from urban centers and crop farms. New regions eclipsed old ones as overgrazing, indiscriminate slaughtering, and the demand for cereals transformed open ranges into regions of hoe and plow agriculture. In some areas the decline was astonishing. Few cattle survived where only a few years earlier cattle had covered the land. By the early seventeenth century, the vast herds of central Mexico were history.[20] In areas of growing population, the need for cereals was especially important in pushing cattle into the peripheral areas. Cities such as Quito responded by reducing common lands for grazing to award more lands for wheat, maize, and barley.[21] Mexico City struggled to limit its common lands to cattle destined for the city market.[22] Soon entire regions began to experience the change. The Bajío in Mexico, a broad, fertile plain that in the 1580s supported large numbers of cattle, sheep, and horses, responded to the rise of Mexico City and the northern silver mining communities by gradually changing from livestock to cereal production.[23]

In the peripheral areas, abundant land and labor shortages made pastoralism a logical activity. As the Caribbean, central Mexico, and the Andes found other uses for land, the *llanos* of Venezuela, the São Francisco River basin of Brazil, the pampas of Argentina, and the far north of Mexico entered phases of expansion. The demand for hides more than anything else fueled the expansion, but diets of New World people benefited as a result.

Meat

Fresh and preserved meats added protein to the diets of rich and poor.[24] Cattle and pigs were so abundant that great roundups took place yearly in the Caribbean to butcher stock, salt flesh, and sell it to the Spanish fleet. Caracas became a center of *tasajo* production, a type of dried and smoked beef consumed by soldiers and sailors. *Cecina* and *charqui* made from layered and salted strips of beef eventually fed the slave populations of

Brazil and the Caribbean.[25] European savants would later criticize the quality of New World meat, but those who knew the land realized how foolish the criticisms were. American meat was just as good and nutritious as European meat.[26]

By the middle of the sixteenth century, almost everybody—Spanish immigrant, English freebooter, Aztec farmer, black slave—ate meat, and plenty of it. Outside Mexico City in the 1550s, as in many other areas, cattle were still slaughtered primarily for their hides. In the city markets, consumers found loin, tongue, kidneys, tripe, sausages, plus lard, cream, milk, and aged, fresh, and curdled cheese. In the broad plains to the north sheep were so abundant and cheap that even a poor man needed a flock of thousands to make a living. Beef was so abundant that laws calling for black slaves and Indians to receive a pound of meat a day were not unrealistic, and were supposedly implemented even on fast days. As part of their daily rations, soldiers in Mexico in the 1580s received two pounds of meat, while those setting out from Spain were lucky to get one pound. Households of the wealthy consumed much meat, at times more than twenty pounds a day. In the simple words of a Peruvian resident, "Meat is dirt cheap in this country."[27]

Pork was as cheap as beef. From the first voyages of discovery, pork—either fresh, salted, or smoked—satisfied the hunger of Europeans. As auxiliaries in the conquest, pigs were more mobile, more adaptable, and hardier than cattle or sheep. They also reproduced faster. In Mexico City in 1526 the price of pork was one-fourth the price in 1524. [28] The reputation of New World pork, already described by the middle of the century as "very sweet and savory, and so wholesome that they give it to sick folks to eat instead of hens and capons" contributed to its appeal.[29] In addition, pigs supplied *manteca de cerdo*, lard that helped to fill the gap left in the Spanish diet by the inadequate supply of olive oil. In regions where beef was scarce, Europeans could at least find pork, often maize-fed, succulent, and comparable to the best European pork.[30]

Although beef and pork were more abundant than in Europe, there were fluctuations in prices and supply. The larger the city, the more commercial and susceptible to interruptions its provisioning system. It is difficult to trace the actual price of meat for consumers in the sixteenth century, but it is possible to show broad trends in the availability of meat. Contract prices for supplying Mexico City with beef and mutton illustrate these trends. After the scarcity of the early years of conquest, prices started to fall by 1528, then plunged in the late 1530s and 1540s to the very low price of about four pounds for one-eighth of a real. These prices shocked foreign observers, who had trouble believing that you could buy a "whole quarter of an oxe, as much as a slave can carry away from the Butchers," for a couple of shillings.[31] With fluctuations, the price stayed low during the 1550s and 1560s, when you could still buy thirty pounds of beef for one real. In the 1570s prices began to climb, holding steady during the 1580s, and then reaching higher in the 1590s. By the end of the century, the price of meat was about double what it had been during the cheapest years, but it was still possible to buy sixteen pounds of beef for one real. Mutton prices followed the same early trends, dropping very low in the 1540s, when mutton was about as cheap as beef, then increasing quickly sometime before 1575, and eventually peaking at about four times the price of beef.[32]

Low prices were the result of available pastures and range lands. Compared to Europe, where there was a delicate balance between tilled, fallow, and pasture land, tropical America had vast pasture lands. In Europe, an increase in livestock forced reduction in grain lands. With low and uncertain yields, such changes threatened subsistence. In Latin America, only a few regions faced similar predicaments: the smaller Caribbean islands and the sugar coast of Brazil, where a law passed in 1701 prohibited cattle raising in the sugar zone within fifty miles of the coast.[33] In central Mexico, demand gradually outpaced supply, leading to a rise in prices, but the rich hinterland and the range lands of the north continued to supply meat through the eighteenth century.

Prices were still low at the end of the century, but for residents accustomed to the cheap beef of the 1550s they were high enough to prompt protest.[34] One cause was the transition to crop agriculture and the northward migration of cattle. The human factor also played a part. Indeed, the shortages that occasionally bothered the city were more the result of inadequacies in the provisioning system than of a shortage of livestock. One problem was the "alliance and confederation" of stockmen, who were determined to drive up the price of meat.[35] Another problem was that beef and mutton prices depended partly on hide and wool prices. With the low prices set for beef, supplies of beef depended on the sale of hides for profit. When hide inventories rose, the availability of beef in the marketplace declined. Consequently, failure of the Atlantic fleet to arrive in Veracruz to pick up hides depressed the price of hides and increased the price of beef. The contradiction of scarcity in the marketplace but abundance of livestock in the country was not lost on contemporaries.[36] Still another problem was the changing consumption pattern of Indians, who ate increasingly large amounts of beef in their villages, thus causing shortages in Mexico City.[37] Officials emphasized another difficulty with Indians: The fighting Chichimecas of the north stole and killed much stock, contributing to the price rise.[38] Two hundred years later Indian raids were still cited as a reason for livestock shortages.[39]

Although these problems disrupted supply, they did not lead to lasting shortages. If meat prices can be believed, Mexico City had adequate if not abundant meat supplies through the century. As prices leveled off and then started to climb, the poor did not have the same choices as earlier, but they still ate meat. They continued to do so in the eighteenth century when Mexico City was the largest city in the hemisphere and had to obtain its meat from long distances. Only now, instead of beef and mutton, the poor ate the flesh of bulls and oxen, described as "tough, difficult to digest, insufferable to the palate, as everybody knows."[40]

How closely other cities followed this pattern is uncertain. Contemporary evidence is often inconsistent and confusing. In Lima, for example, stock damaged gardens and fields as in other areas, leading to complaints of too many cattle. Yet urban residents worried about shortages of meat, and laws were passed to protect breeding stock.[41] Without specific prices, the complaints tell us little except that supply might have been more unstable than in Mexico City.. Even when price information is available, as for Guatemala City in the late sixteenth century, it is difficult to determine how much meat was actually available.[42] It seems likely that cities went through their own cycles of change that roughly paralleled developments in Mexico City. Early scarcity turned into abundant supplies that declined as demand grew and pasture lands became crop lands.

Without pressure from growing population centers, meat was virtually free, left to rot or burned after butchering.[43] In the eighteenth century people in the cattle zones continued to consume enormous amounts of beef. Cowboys in Argentina ate meat three times a day, washed down with maté. In Paraguay, butchers were not needed because the "poorer sort do not buy pounds of meat, as is customary in Europe, but a part of a slaughtered ox." The only kitchen utensil in the home of the poor was an iron rod slanted toward the fire, the spit for cooking endless amounts of beef. Cows were killed daily and their meat hung from corral posts so hungry workers could cut away what they wanted.[44]

In the sweep of Latin American history, the sixteenth century interrupted the general trend of a decline in consumption of animal protein. With the advent of agriculture and the formation of sedentary communities in Mesoamerica and the Andes, cereals and tubers fed more and more people, while hunting and fishing yielded smaller returns. Nomadic peoples, skilled at gathering and taking sufficient nutrients from the environment, gave way to peoples living in large, complex communities, dependent on the more intensive use of limited resources. The trend culminated around 1500, when intensive crop agriculture supported millions of people.

After the conquest, ranching overshadowed crop farming, returning meat to a primary place in the diet. The sixteenth century altered the trend, but did not break it. Except in the cattle regions, the cheap meat of the sixteenth century gradually increased in price as populations recovered and crop agriculture displaced ranching. In the twentieth century, the diet of most Indians more closely resembled that of the fifteenth than of the sixteenth century. Meat as daily fare was once again a luxury.

Wheat

Wheat cultivation was more demanding than stock raising. The return on wheat for effort expended was smaller and more susceptible to loss than the return on livestock. Wheat, which was used mainly for flour for bread, was less versatile than cattle, which yielded hides, soap, and tallow in addition to meat. Labor requirements for tilling, sowing, and harvesting were greater than for stock raising. Capital investments in the land, especially irrigation in regions of inadequate rainfall, increased the expense of wheat farming. Land ownership, or at least tighter control over land, usually preceded the new investments. Transportation networks built around ships, canoes, carts, and mule trains added to the cost. So did the construction of mills for turning the wheat into flour and ovens for turning flour into bread.[45]

Despite the expense and obstacles, Spaniards planted wheat with an intensity lacking with other crops. Wheat was a cultural imperative, a driving force that shaped the social and physical landscape. Where wheat was planted and survived, Spanish society took root and grew. Early chroniclers noted with satisfaction the production of wheat, making comparisons with Spain when particularly good breads were made. The lack of wheat was just as important to note, for without it Spaniards lost a valued part of their culture.[46]

Other essential foods in the sixteenth-century Spanish diet—such as mutton, wine, and olive oil—gradually lost their importance as other foods replaced them in the New World. This was not the case with wheat, which might have been more available in Spanish America than in Spain. In Spain the availability of wheat declined as rye and barley emerged as substitutes. Already by 1503, the crown tried to peg the price of wheat at 110 maravedis the *fanega*, followed by rye at 70 and barley at 60.[47] In talking about the decline of Spain in the seventeenth century, Alvarez Ossorio y Redín made sure to refer to the many who ate barley bread, a food for the poor.[48] By the end of the eighteenth century, wheat production (32 million *fanegas*) just surpassed the combined total of barley, rye, and maize (31 million).[49] Perhaps Spaniards immigrating to America appreciated wheat so much because of its increasing scarcity on the peninsula. The scarcity of wheat and its association with an admired and sought-after way of life was general throughout Europe.[50] Most people ate gruel or hard breads made from rye, barley, spelt, or maslin. In America, Spaniards ate a staple that was scarce in Europe.

Maize did not undercut the early cultural preference for wheat, despite being proclaimed "worthy of the highest praise and glory, fit for Spaniards and Indians, sick and healthy, men and women."[51] Some saw it as an "excellent food," neither hot nor cold, easy to sow and harvest. They debunked the belief that it caused obstructions, arguing that when it was prepared as *atole* (maize gruel) it was comparable to the barley broths recommended by Hippocrates.[52]

Laudatory assessments did not convince most Europeans. John Gerard, the famous though not always most reliable sixteenth-century herbalist, summed up their thinking, calling maize "a more convenient food for swine than for men," since it had little bran, was hard to digest, and gave little nourishment.[53] Spaniards had already recognized the virtues of maize for fodder. Oviedo carefully described the methods of planting and harvesting and the many ways that Indians prepared maize. He then noted that Spaniards found it very good for livestock.[54] Similar opinions helped to slow the spread of maize in Europe, but hunger has a way of ignoring scholarly appraisals. By the end of the seventeenth century, large numbers of poor in Asturias, Galicia, Vizcaya, Málaga, and Granada ate breads and gruels made from maize.[55]

Texture and consistency had a lot to do with European dislike of maize and preference for wheat. In the sixteenth century, sailors complained of receiving their rations of maize in kernels, instead of ground, like wheat. Difficulties of digestion were attributed to maize.[56] Three hundred years later the same complaints were heard. Maize was still milled by hand and ground in *metates*, whereas wheat was milled by machine, producing a smooth, fine flour. When maize was carefully ground, there was agreement that it produced a better-tasting, more nutritious bread.[57]

The commitment to wheat could not overcome the climatic difficulties of the islands. Efforts to plant wheat in the islands failed, reducing them to dependence on the mainland.[58] In parts of Mexico, and then in the Andes, wheat grew well. First planted in the Valley of Mexico soon after the fall of Tenochtitlán, wheat spread quickly, yielding abundant harvests by 1530.[59] By 1563 at least 114 farms produced wheat in the central valley.[60] As Spanish society pushed outward from Mexico City, colonizers planted wheat in other valleys, and then in the plains of the north. The richest producer was the valley of Puebla, where some communities supposedly produced 70,000 to 80,000 *fanegas* a year. In the town of Atlixco, near Puebla, the harvest reached 100,000 *fanegas* in the early seventeenth century. Such totals were exceptional. Adequate water, fertile soils, and a good climate led to estimates of the very high production ratios of one hundred to one. With luck, it was even possible to have three harvests a year, in June, October, and early spring. More important was the regularity of production, which seldom failed, according to comtemporaries.[61] In the late eighteenth century, when demands for wheat were much heavier, there was still little concern for successive harvest failures. Only very rarely, once every thirty to fifty years, did one bad harvest follow another.[62]

To the north, the valley stretching from Querétaro to Guadalajara emerged as a major producer by the end of the century. Sporadic water supplies and more dramatic weather changes threatened yields, but did not prevent the growth of the region as a primary grain producer. Fingers of production extended farther north, following the *camino real* toward the mines. Some regions became important in their own right, but few matched the surplus production of central Mexico.[63]

In the Andean region, wheat encountered more obstacles than in Mexico. Along the arid coastal strip wheat did not germinate without irrigation; in the high mountain reaches above 12,000 feet it did not grow at all. In between, in the valleys around Quito, Riobamba, Cuenca, Cajamarca, Chachapoyas, Guánuco, Guamanga, Cuzco, Arequipa, and dozens of other smaller valleys to the north and south, enough wheat was produced to ship to other areas.[64] Some small coastal communities survived only because of the trade in flour.[65] It was the active trade in flour that fed grain-dependent cities like Lima and Potosí. For the region as a whole, one observer noted that Peru could produce a ten-year supply of grain in one year if it were not for the problems of spoilage.[66] As in Mexico, shortages were unusual, occurring maybe two or three times in every thirty years.[67]

Bread

Spaniards first ate bread in the form of *bizcocho*, the dry, hard wafers later known as *galletas*. Dependence on the imported *bizcocho* continued until after the turmoil of conquest, when farms began producing wheat. Military men continued eating *bizcocho*, but by the middle of the sixteenth century, fresh bread fed most Europeans. Bread continued to gain importance, accompanying Spaniards north and south as they founded new towns. While many of the sights and smells of the New World bewildered visitors, they could usually count on fresh-baked bread in the Iberian tradition to remind them of home.

As markets for bread expanded, the types of bread increased, serving different social groups. By the end of the sixteenth century in Mexico City, *pan blanco* (white bread) was almost twice as expensive as *semita*, a coarse bread eaten by the poor.[68] As the colonial period drew to a close, four types of wheat bread (*francés, floreado, común, baso*), each associated with a particular social and economic group, fed Mexico City.[69] Bread responded to changing social and economic conditions in Europe in much the same way.[70] The main difference was that in Latin America the very poor, usually Indians, ate maize breads, while in Europe the poor ate breads made from barley and rye.

Most wheat produced was shipped to urban centers, ground in mills, sold to bakers, turned into bread, then distributed to consumers. How much bread was actually consumed, and how it contributed to dietary patterns, is difficult to ascertain. There are few specific contemporary references to the availability of bread in the sixteenth century, which makes it more difficult to generalize about bread than about meat. From estimates of local flour production it is possible to calculate bread production, once the conversion rate of flour to bread is known. For example, in Potosí in 1603, 28 bakeries used 250 *fanegas* of flour daily, baking bread at one real per pound for a total value of 18 pesos per *fanega*. At 8 reales per peso, this meant 144 pounds of bread per *fanega*, or 36,000 pounds of bread per day.[71] Conversion rates of wheat to bread are also available. The *cabildo* of Lima received a report in 1553 stating that each *fanega* of wheat, "limpio y fecho harina," produced 120 pounds of bread. In seventeenth-century Spain, each *fanega* of wheat gave only 70 pounds of bread.[72] Taking the 70-pound figure, the valley of Atlixco could produce 700,000 pounds of bread per year, enough for 2 pounds per day for 1,000 people. Other figures could be given. What they suggest is the potential for the consumption of large amounts of wheat bread.

Bread prices give further evidence. Bread prices, like meat prices, declined soon after conquest. By the end of the 1520s in Mexico City, a bread-processing system was securely in place, resulting in a drop in prices. One-pound loaves dropped from eight to four maravedis in the two years after 1529, then continued their decline until 1539, when one tomín (thirty-four maravedis) bought sixteen pounds, about half the price of 1531. This bread was supposedly "white, clean, well cooked and seasoned," and not mixed with barley and sand.[73] After that, irregular and gradually increasing prices characterized the trade until the 1550s, a decade of very high prices compared to earlier years. It is hard to say whether bread prices were increasing at a faster rate than other foodstuffs, since the decade of the 1550s was one of a generalized price increase in New Spain.[74] By the 1590s prices were higher than ever before, but by that time the much cheaper bread of *semitas* was on the marketplace. One real bought seven pounds of the *semitas* or four pounds or less of white bread.[75]

It is clear that there was more irregularity in the price of bread than of meat. Signs of trouble in bread provisioning appeared before the 1550s. Bakers (*panaderos*) short-weighted bread, used improper ingredients, or charged unfair prices until forced to sell their bread in the *plaza mayor*. Mills broke down or were monopolized, leading to higher prices. Frosts curtailed harvests, prompting laws forbidding the shipping of wheat and bread outside of the city. Indians failed to fulfill their tribute quotas of grain to the city. Officials took on the responsibility of monitoring supplies and prices, but even with adequate supplies of grain, shortages still led to higher prices.[76] After the 1550s, Mexico City continued its administrative efforts to ensure a regular supply of bread. To increase supplies, it pressured Indians to plant more wheat and initiated efforts to open roads to other wheat areas. Loans from the viceroy allowed the city to reach farther into the countryside for grain.[77] While moving to stabilize its own supply of bread, Mexico City continued to ship flour and hardtack to Veracruz and Havana. It was able to do so even during times of wheat shortages because of abundant supplies of maize.[78] The many piecemeal efforts to provision bread were part of the general centralization of control over food provisioning, which culminated in the creation of public markets and warehouses.

Lima seemed frustrated by the same problems as Mexico City, despite a downward trend in prices after the conquest. Prices could drop sharply. In 1549 one peso bought twenty-two pounds of bread; in 1551 one peso bought thirty-six pounds. Contemporaries thought bread was cheap, and noted that many Indians and poor ate it, but this did not silence critics of the bread trade.[79] The problems were familiar. Producers resisted selling grains, hoping to monopolize the baking and selling of bread. When grain was sold, intermediaries escalated prices, contributing to the uncertainty of supply. Bakers were not faultless, as they short-weighted bread and refused to follow price schedules. As Lima emerged as a grain and hardtack entrepôt, supplies were further limited. When the valleys of Chancay and Guaura shipped flour to Tierra Firme, shortages resulted in Lima.[80] More damaging was the earthquake of 1586, which threatened the future production and distribution of grain.[81]

Bread supplies in Mexico City and Lima were more erratic than meat supplies. Whether consumers experienced lasting shortages as a result is another matter. Producers had to sell their wheat, and the drop in prices in the first areas of settlement shows much competition for markets. The main producing regions of central Mexico, the temperate Andean basins, and central Chile produced such surpluses that external markets (usually limited to other colonial towns with modest populations until the late eighteenth century) were necessary for survival. At least as early as 1583 the Lima *cabildo* noted with interest the cheap and abundant wheat supplies of Chile. The eastern Bajío shipped carloads of wheat, along with wool and mutton, to Mexico City by 1590.[82] Even with the urban markets, wheat from the provinces was at times left piled in sacks, unguarded, exposed to the weather, rotting.[83] It was this contradiction between wheat surpluses and urban scarcity that made the politics of food so controversial.

Meat, Bread, and Colonization

The irregularity of bread prices and the frequent complaints of shortages do not prove that widespread food shortages existed. In Spanish America, the bread-meat relationship that dominated most world food regimes did not apply. In traditional agricultural societies, population growth required the increased consumption of grains and tubers. Grazing lands and fodder limited the production of crops for human consumption, forcing a reallocation of resources. Since land used for crops could support many times the population of land used for livestock, pasture lands were converted to crop lands in sixteenth-century Europe.[84] If this had not been done, the already uncertain provisioning system would have been further threatened. In early Spanish America, the land use question was less important. Increased production came through the introduction of Spanish crops and livestock into new areas, not through a reallocation of resources. The availability of land for livestock, aided by the tragic decline of the Indian population in the central areas, more than anything else distinguished New World from European agriculture.

A comparison of meat and bread prices in Mexico City during years of bread shortages illustrates the New World's freedom from the bread-meat relationship. As mentioned, in the 1550s one real bought four pounds of bread, while one real bought about thirty pounds of meat. By the 1590s, bread will still four times as expensive as meat. Wheat bread was expensive compared to meat, while the opposite was true in most of Europe. This fact overturns the usual interpretations of diet and income. The poor, rather than being forced to subsist on breads and gruels, had meat as a basic foodstuff. As their income increased, they had more choice, and perhaps consumed more wheat products.

Furthermore, emphasis on increasing wheat and bread prices minimizes the diversity and availability of other foodstuffs in the marketplace and the diet. As bread prices increased in the large urban centers, other foods became more attractive. In Lima, when the price of wheat was too high, the poor could always eat cassava, potatoes, and other root crops.[85] The nonmeat foods available in Mexico City markets by the 1550s included: fresh and saltwater fish, chickpeas, lentils, beans, lettuce, radishes, turnips, carrots, dates, raisins, rice, almonds, filberts, various fruits, and herbs, plus confections and preserves made from vegetables and fruits.[86] To complete the list, many nutritious New World foods would have to be mentioned. This diversity supports the contention that there was an adequate supply of food.

All of these foods contributed nutrients that helped Spain conquer and colonize the New World. Local foods predominated as Spaniards pushed out from the Caribbean and penetrated the highlands of Mexico and Peru. These foods quieted physical cravings, but did not satisfy cultural expectations of the ideal Spanish diet. Only wheat and meat could do this. Soon the towns and cities that sprang up as Spaniards moved north and south tried to establish their own sources of supply of wheat and meat. Those that were successful became centers of the Spanish presence in the New World.

Laws and Institutions

Europeans arrived in the New World with definite ideas about the politics of food. They recognized that laws and institutions affected food supplies as much as did climate and soil. There is little doubt that the politics of food was at least as important in the past as it is today. Producers wanted subsidies and import restrictions; processors and distributors complained of costly regulation; consumers demanded low prices; and governments worried about the loyalty of populations inadequately fed. Today, when the discussion of scarcity has finally become more a political question than an agricultural one, we have rediscovered what residents of Latin America appreciated long ago.

The politics of food was a daily concern that influenced life in many ways. Domínguez y Compañy summarized one viewpoint: "The politics of provisioning the city was without doubt, along with the regulation of prices, the problem that most preoccuppied local colonial government in Latin America."[1] City officials worried about many other things—constructing buildings, aqueducts, and wells; paying salaries and bills; awarding lands;

defining political jurisdictions—depending on time and circumstance. Thoughts of food, though, were never far from their minds. There was a general awareness of food as a moral issue, and a belief that government had an obligation to provide for the needs of the community. This was part of a wider commitment to an ideal community that would perpetuate the Spanish way of life. Juan de Ovando, president of the Council of the Indies, wrote in his *Book of Spiritual Governance* (1571) that since God had entrusted Spain with so many kingdoms, it was Spain's obligation to provide "bread, wine, oil, cloth, silks, linens, horses, cattle, arms and tools, to work and cultivate the land."[2] Two years later, regulations outlined the perfect community, complete with the oxen, horses, sheep, chickens, and grains necessary for survival.[3]

As ideal and reality clashed, food emerged as a political issue. It was an important issue, but it did not have the overarching significance in the New World that it semed to have in some regions of Europe. Steven Kaplan has commented that provisioning "dominated life in old regime Europe in a merciless and unremitting way. No issue was more urgent, more pervasively felt, and more difficult to resolve than the matter of grain provisioning."[4] Only in exceptional times was the Spanish American situation as serious as this. The evidence is not strong enough to prove that crisis after crisis plagued the colonies, turning the politics of food into the politics of survival.

Instead, the politics of food unfolded as one part of the process of colonization. In the first years, many of the basic mechanisms for provisioning were put into place. Later conditions forced adaptations and changes, but these seldom altered the nature of the politics of food. Environment and society created some regional diversity, but the Spanish origins of food regulation dictated that institutions and laws would be similar through most of Spanish America. Since there was an adequate supply of many of the staples, politics revolved around their distribution, not their production. The rhetoric of food at times emphasized the issue of subsistence, but after the first years of settlement food surpluses often reduced it to secondary importance. Food as nutrients, necessary for life and health, was often less important than food as income and power. The interplay between producers, distributors, consumers, and political officials, each struggling to further their own interests, gave life to the politics of food.

The Early Years

Colonial policy originated in the directives that the Catholic monarchs gave to Columbus. The monarchs, especially Isabella, a woman with a fine administrative flair, must have had a feeling of excitement, a sense of a new and glorious adventure about to unfold. Spanish monarchs were no strangers to incorporating territory, something that they had done in earnest during the reconquest. But the Columbus enterprise was something different: the exploration of a new world full of strange plants, animals, men, and customs, a land far from home that lacked much that Europeans considered essential for happiness.

An acceptable food supply was basic to establishing a colony on Hispaniola and for reaching out to other islands. Despite the fertility of the soil and the profusion of foods noted by Columbus, future colonists demanded more.[5] They demanded foods with familiar flavors and consistencies. Cultural associations and tastes intervened at an early period, prompting a food policy designed to provision the islands with Spanish foods. The policy eventually led to the self-sufficiency of many colonies.

At first, the crown assumed much of the responsibility for provisioning, as an extension of its support for the voyages of discovery. At royal expense, thousands of sacks of wheat flour and barrels of hardtack, along with jar after jar of wine, vinegar, and olive oil, went to Hispaniola. In spite of the shortages in Andalusia at the time, enough rations and provisions were acquired for the early settlement of the island. At the same time that the crown drew from its own resources, it encouraged merchants to buy in Spain for resale in the new markets.[6] From the beginning, the crown and private enterprise interacted to influence the food history of America.

As Admiral of the Ocean Sea, Columbus enjoyed vast privileges. The monarchs entrusted him with the details of provisioning, from acquiring food for voyages to distributing rations in Hispaniola. At the same time that they were trying to regulate grain prices at home, they gave Columbus the authority to control the production and distribution of food. Specifically, he had the power to set agricultural prices "so that there will be some profit . . . and the people will not suffer."[7] How high the profit should be was not stated. In the eighteenth century, custom dictated a maximum 12.5 percent profit on "commerce of first necessity."[8] When merchants balked at putting foods on the market in the hope of forcing prices up and profiting from early agricultural failures, Columbus had the legal authority to force them to send goods to market. His inability to crack the trading monopolies, however, contributed to the early shortages that the island experienced.[9]

Crown officials struggled to ease the shortages and weaken the food traffickers. They did so at first by responding to particular conditions rather than by establishing uniform policies. In some cases, their concern was for "honest and moderate prices"; in other cases, it was to protect merchants, even if this meant letting them sell at the prices "they wanted and could get." Without this incentive, it was thought, merchants would stop shipping food to the Indies. At one moment merchants enjoyed a privileged, protected position; at another, all colonists could traffic in food. Conflicting food laws were a part of early settlement.[10]

Agriculture was as important to food policy as were price regulation and distribution. Through Columbus, the crown encouraged an agricultural system that would produce the staples essential to the Spanish diet. A self-sufficient colony was envisioned after the second voyage. The scope of the vision was staggering: nothing short of recreating the agricultural and alimentary life of Spain on a still-unknown island. Undaunted by the magnitude of the project and unaware of many of the obstacles, colonizers and administrators planned the future of the colony. Colonization now entailed the careful packaging and shipping of seeds and cuttings for wheat, barley, olives, grapes, and dozens of common vegetables and fruits. Along with the plants went animals such as cattle, sheep, pigs, goats, oxen, and horses, and tools such as hoes, rakes, and plows.[11] Later conquerors urged the same attention for their newly taken lands. In a letter to Charles V, Hernán Cortés suggested that no ship leave Spain without bringing plants for farming.[12]

Enthusiasm for agricultural productivity in the islands was not matched in Spain, where the crown was mortgaging the agricultural future for quick profits from wool. In 1501 a land-lease law in Spain crippled politically weak farmers by allowing sheepmen to rent lands they already held at current prices for an indefinite time. In addition, sheepmen could control lands already occupied without the consent of owners. Vicens Vives captured the historical significance: "There is something here, a negative element that must have been very deeply rooted, which strikes very deep in Castilian economic history and explains the anguish of farmers."[13]

Conflicts between ranchers and farmers occurred in the New World, but never to the same extent nor with the same disastrous consequences as in Spain. One reason was that early policy was more constructive. In 1529, for example, the crown ordered the shipment of different types of wheat to Cuba, specifying with a revealing awareness of farmers' needs that it should arrive on time for planting. In 1531, Charles V promised immigrant farmers free passage, food, land, stock, Indian labor, exemption from tithes, and lands for their descendants. In 1535, the crown encouraged New Spain, a land already reputed "rich in grain," to sow enough for the islands. This order anticipated Mexico's emergence as a major grain exporter.[14] A more telling reason for the success of crop farming over ranching was the pasture and prairie land that stretched endlessly beyond settlements.

Agriculture was influenced by the conflicting demands for nutrients and exportable wealth. The colonies could not survive unless they produced their own food. Spain, already a food importer, had little to offer except specialty foods and beverages. The Canary Islands continued to ship flour, hardtack, conserves, and cheeses, but not enough to supply the needs of colonial society.[15] The political implications were evident. In the words of the great seventeenth-century Spanish jurist Solórzano y Pereyra, food and agriculture were the basis of "the glory, population, and sovereignty of kingdoms; lacking food, they are depopulated and reduced to deserts."[16]

The Laws of Burgos (1512–13), the first attempt to codify the relations between Indians and Spaniards, spelled out the agricultural obligations of the new masters, requiring plantings of maize, cassava, sweet potatoes, chiles, and the raising of chickens. Portugal had similar laws for Brazil, insisting that owners of slaves and slave ships plant cassava and maintain food reserves.[17] The use of forced labor for the production of subsistence foods was not seriously questioned since the vitality of the colonies depended upon it. Agricultural workers had to supply nonagricultural workers with food. Later, the need for good food in the mines was stressed. All needed to eat well, since worker productivity depended on health, and health depended on diet.[18]

The political struggle over provisioning began with Columbus. Some of the conflicts and contradictions in the struggle had emerged before the colony was ten years old. Inherent in crown policy was a paternalistic, medieval notion of the state as provider and protector that clashed with the mercantilist objectives of the imperial state. Food policy, and the willingness to enforce it, was usually tempered by powerful economic forces. New private interests, some of them protected by the crown, began to participate in the processing and distribution of food. Motivated by their own pecuniary interests, merchants, and soon butchers, bakers, and candle makers, were accused of violating the special trust that allowed them to deal in goods vital to the public welfare. The conflict between public good and private gain erupted early and remained one of the central issues in the political history of food. The regulatory agencies and pricing procedures established in Spanish America were one effort to resolve the conflict.

Policies and Procedures

The political organization of food that eventually emerged was like a honeycomb, composed of many separate but interlocking compartments, each fulfilling a similar function but responding to different influences. As problems of provisioning became more complex, the food bureaucracy increased in size, swelling the ranks of town government. Soon the main centers of empire had broadly similar practices for regulating the essential goods consumed in the city. Though provisioning remained an imperial concern, the politics of food was a local matter. After the Columbus years, the biological and political survival of the colonies depended more on what happened in the developing urban centers of the New World than in Spain.

It is not easy to summarize the many conflicting interests and agencies that influenced food in the sixteenth century. In the beginning, the *cabildo*, the main organization for urban government, assumed responsibility for provisioning. As need arose, cities petitioned for the establishment of *fieles ejecutorías* within the *cabildo*. These were staffed by *fieles ejecutores*, charged with taking care of urban food needs. Santo Domingo, Mexico City, San Cristóbal, Santiago de Guatemala, Granada, León, Nombre de Dios, Panama, and Lima all had the right to a *fiel ejecutoría* by 1550, although negotiations over the precise powers of the *fiel* might continue for years.[19] In the big cities, the *fiel* was flanked by many deputies, administrators, managers, and measurers for meat, wheat, maize, mills, slaughterhouses, and common lands.[20] The food bureaucracy seemed almost more complex than the system of provisioning by the end of the century.

The *fiel ejecutor* was the most important urban food officer. With origins deep in the past, perhaps in the food ediles of Rome, the office of *fiel* had a secure place in Spanish institutional life and was quickly transported to the colonies. Mexico City elected its first *fiel* in 1524. His function, which first was to supervise weights and measures and oversee stores, evolved into "intervening in everything referring to the provisioning of the city."[21] In practice, this meant early trips to fish markets; the testing of salts, oils, and soaps; the struggle to keep streets and markets clean; the regulation of new construction; control over profits and fines; continual negotiations with producers and distributors, and more.

Need for the *fiel* was based on the principle that all within the city should have access to good food at a fair price. An unregulated system of production and distribution left consumers at the mercy of the powerful. To reduce the nutritional gap that might result, the *fiel* pursued different strategies. He strove to keep food transactions open to public scrutiny. He did so by actually visiting as many shops as he could, varying the times of visits in the hope of catching transgressors. Shortages were caused by the many intermediaries—sometimes goods passed through five or six hands—who profited from the food trade.[22] To avoid "the secret selling which led to the harm and detriment of the republic," the regraters and forestallers, commonly known as *regatones*, had to be controlled.[23] High prices resulted from the frequent exchange of goods or from the opposite, the hoarding of goods. Either way, *regatones* were accused of "destroying this republic."[24] They were even accused of causing more shortages than the weather.[25]

The *fiel* addressed the problem by regulating prices and quality through the use of *posturas* and *aranceles*, which were widely accepted though seldom clearly defined methods of control. Both sought to limit excessive profits by establishing prices for goods of common consumption. By the middle of the sixteenth century, *posturas* regulated the price of meats, fruits, nuts, cheeses, beverages, and fish. When conditions warranted, they were also established for carrots, radishes, and cabbages.[26] Special *posturas* and *aranceles* applied to inns for merchants and travelers, the *ventas* in Mexico and the *tambos* in Peru. For trade to prosper, merchants needed adequate quantities of food and fodder at fair prices.[27] If evidence from the seventeenth century applies to the sixteenth, determining food prices was an involved process, embracing conflicting groups who often accused their competitors of duplicity and fraud. The livelihood of wholesalers and retailers depended on the relationship between expenses and earnings. It was in this microcosm of the price of fish, beans, grains, and honey that the *fiel* helped to determine the food destiny of the emerging colonies.[28]

Another strategy, seen in the sixteenth century but more widespread by the eighteenth, was to separate processing and distribution activities. Thus bakers could not be millers, and shopkeepers could not bake bread. In a similar manner, those who slaughtered stock could not infringe on the occupation of the butchers, and neither of these could buy tallow, which was reserved for candlemakers.[29] Maintaining the integrity of professions had more than a nutritional objective by the eighteenth century. In just about every phase of production, from coarse textiles to fancy pastries, unlicensed producers who ignored pricing and quality regulations threatened the established producers. The potential for conflict was enormous, giving added importance to the role of the *fiel* as an economic mediator.[30]

Here was regulation in the extreme, a bureaucratic impulse consistent with the image of the state as arbitrator of the provisioning system. Regulation went beyond the city to encompass the relationship between city and country. New pressures on the environment threatened to deplete food-related resources. Responses differed according to conditions, but there were some widely held concerns. In both Mexico City and Lima, forests, pasture lands, and water resources commanded much attention. Stripping the forests deprived cities of fuel and hastened erosion. Overcrowded and inadequate pasture lands increased the price of meat. Too much or too little water choked agricultural life. In response, cities passed laws to manage their resources.[31]

The *fiel* and others could do little to ensure adherence to environmental and food distribution laws. When the term of office was short, one month in Lima in the 1550s, the *fiel* had little chance of success.[32] Voluntary compliance was too much to expect, especially since the retail and wholesale trade in food supported so many Indians and Spaniards. Profits were so high that many became *regatones* instead of going into other trades.[33] Energetic and responsive officials did curtail some abuses, but the continual complaints against *regatones* suggest a problem that lasted through the colonial period.[34]

It was as difficult to collect taxes on food as it was to regulate prices and distribution. The *diezmo*, levied on the production of grains, vegetables, meats, and processed foods, was the most widely enforced tax. From Hispaniola in 1501, the tax followed Spaniards to other islands and the mainland, where it met with grudging acceptance. Many more objections delayed the implementation of the *alcabala*, despite the agreement by jurists that it was an ancient right of the king of Castile. By 1558, the decision was made to apply it to the new lands, and finally after hesitation and regional opposition the tax was introduced into Mexico in the 1570s and Peru in the 1590s.[35] Many rules and exemptions governed the *alcabala*, but usually it was a tax of two percent on agricultural goods produced and exchanged. Maize for Indian consumption and foods sold in public markets were significant exemptions.[36] Although confusion continued to surround the *alcabala*, it had been imposed through much of Spanish America by the end of the sixteenth century. Even in Quito, where opposition to the tax almost led to rebellion in 1592, officials could report in 1595 that they collected it with ease.[37] The *almojarifazgo* was another tax. It applied to goods imported from Spain and to some interregional trading. At times the rate of the *almojarifazgo* far surpassed that of the *diezmo* and *alcabala*, as in the 20 percent tax imposed on wine in Mexico beginning in 1526.[38] Protests and delays were an ongoing part of the history of these taxes, which could add up to 66 percent of the value of goods, without the *alcabala*.[39]

Special taxes also influenced the food supply. By 1540, Mexico City had permission to levy a tax on selected foodstuffs. Three years later this tax, known as the *sisa*, was collected on meat. Later, in 1583, the *sisa* was shifted to wine.[40] In Lima, the *sisa* on meat caused concern for the diet of the poor, but did not lead to the complete elimination of the tax. In one year in the seventeenth century, the tax on meat, including the *sisa* and the *alcabala*, amounted to 37 percent.[41] Still another type of tax was the *composición*, a fixed charge for confirmation of land titles and the right to sell goods, use water, and the like. The history of the *composición* in the sixteenth century is not well known, but by the eighteenth century it had become a serious problem, provoking outrage among the *pulperos*, small shopkeepers who argued that the tax threatened their survival.[42]

These taxes and procedures caused interminable conflicts as officials attempted to balance concern for nutritional well-being, the rights of producers and distributors, and the financial needs of the state. The conflicts were simply another variant of the broader dialectic of Spanish American politics. Ever hopeful of meeting what they perceived as a fundamental duty, regulatory agencies sought to limit prices without discouraging production, to organize and simplify distribution without depriving anyone of an income, and to ensure that the consumer had adequate food without limiting the taxes collected by city and crown.

For most food issues, it was enough just to stymie the flagrant abusers of the system and pass laws to protect the consumers. Food politics limped along in this fashion. What it all meant for food supplies is another matter. Only infrequently was the system criticized as being the cause of shortages. That taxes on food were imposed so readily, especially the *sisa* on meat, suggests adequate supplies. When taxes and procedures led to unrest, the effect on occupations and incomes, not food and health, was usually the reason. Thus organized responses to food laws came from *pulperos*, pork merchants, and fishmongers—people who saw their livelihood threatened.[43]

Public Markets

Meat and grain required their own institutions. More than a response to local supplies, the new institutions represented the desire to re-create in the New World patterns of life at home. Fence posts were sunk for corrals, foundations laid for buildings, bins constructed for grains, ordinances written for food officials. Out of the efforts emerged the *albóndiga, pósito*, and *abasto de carne*.

The gradual centralization of grain policies culminated in the creation of *alhóndigas*, controlled markets for grains. According to theory, the sale of grains in a public market, under the supervision of municipal officials, on city property, and with a published schedule of prices, would eliminate abuses. The Lima *cabildo* decided to build an *alhóndiga* in 1555.[44] Mexico City reclaimed land in 1567 for an *alhóndiga*, issued ordinances for operation in 1580, and started buying and selling in 1581.[45] Not everyone celebrated the event. A treasury official sided with the wheat farmers who opposed the *alhóndiga*, stating that the crown would lose some 8,000 pesos in taxes.[46] Later evidence suggests that small shopkeepers also opposed the *alhóndiga* since it deprived them of a principal trade item.[47] Political conflict surrounded the *alhóndiga* from the beginning.

Supporters proceeded on the principle that the stricter the regulations, the more successful would be the control of grains. Original plans usually called for the sale of maize, wheat, and barley in the *alhóndiga*, and a detailed listing of who could buy how much, when, and at what price. In fact, the particular conditions of time and place, supply and demand, influenced grain policy. In both Mexico City and Lima grain continued to be traded outside the market. Lima officials in particular had a difficult time regulating the grains brought in by sea and then transferred to the provinces. In Trujillo, to the north of Lima, problems were more severe as Spaniards, mestizos, and blacks profited from the illegal bread trade.[48]

Measured against its objectives, the *alhóndiga* failed. It never monopolized distribution and pricing, primarily because of inadequate financing and ineffective enforcement. Too many people produced and consumed grain for municipalities to oversee provisioning. Recognition of the difficulties prompted debate in Lima in 1561 on whether to abolish the *alhóndiga* and permit the unrestricted sale of grain.[49] In the 1590s there was again discussion of appropriate ways to distribute grain imported from Chile. Some recommended the free sale of grain, others recommended limits. Still others thought that a price should be imposed that would generate enough profit to help the poor and at the same time allow the city to buy more grain reserves.[50] More evidence on these debates would reveal much about sixteenth-century political philosophy. About all that can be said at this point is that the system of distribution that was taking shape did not go unchallenged. By the end of the colonial period the challenges became more widespread as the entire apparatus of food control was criticized.[51]

In the late sixteenth century, more control, rather than less, was needed. It took the form of the *pósito*, or grain storehouse. Once again, the issue was supply, not production. Despite the good harvests of grain around

Mexico City in 1592 and 1593, little grain appeared in the market. To get the grain to market, the viceroy ordered officials into the countryside to look for supplies of wheat and flour and impound them for the city.[52] Traditionalists believed the only solution was for the city to buy grain, store it, and set prices in the public market. Earlier proposals for this had not been carried out because it had not "appeared to be necessary."[53] It was also difficult, much more so than running the *alhóndiga*. It required prudence and commitment, virtues that generally good grain supplies did not promote.[54] The same dilemma faced Mexico City two centuries later, when the city's grain demands were much heavier. As mentioned, successive bad harvests were very unusual. Even after the disastrous famine of 1785–86, there was not enough support for public control over wheat. Farmers, millers, and bakers continued to act as the guardians of the viceroyalty's grain supply. Cries that the lack of a *pósito* for wheat threatened the realm led to new ideas and a renewed interest in the original proposal of 1580. The colonial memory was a long one, but jarring it had little effect. There was just too much wheat available to justify the expense of a *pósito*.[55]

The *abasto de carne*, the meat supply system, complemented the *alhóndiga* and *pósito*. Ideally, the *abasto* was a semi-public enterprise, where public responsibility was fulfilled while private initiative was rewarded. In principle, the meat contractor, known as the *obliqado*, at times alternating with private stockmen, supplied the city with meat for a year or longer at a stipulated price. In practice, complete disorder seemed to reign as consumers complained about short-weighted, diseased, and rancid meats. The Lima *abasto*, which at times found itself without an *obligado*, was especially notorious for its chaos and inefficiency.[56]

The size and complexity of the *abasto* undermined the best of intentions. Salaried agents bought cattle and sheep, hired assistants, and then drove the stock to pastures or corrals on the outskirts of the city. From there, the stock went to slaughterhouses, then the meat was transferred in carts to butcher shops. Arrangements were made for the marketing of tallow, hides, and viscera. Salaries for accountants, laborers, and administrators had to be paid at every stage. Equipment was purchased and taxes paid. In Mexico City in the 1570s, total expenses for supplying the city with beef and mutton exceeded 150,000 pesos a year, a mighty sum for one individual. The city hesitated to assume the burden directly. When it did so, losses could follow.[57] There was not enough profit in meat to compensate for unexpected losses or for breakdowns in the marketing of cattle and sheep byproducts.

In the provinces matters were worse. *Abastos* were a part of the general pattern of colonization and were found in many Indian communities by the 1570s. A complete disregard of prices, and an apparently unending violation of regulations, quickly caught the notice of viceroys in Mexico City. New procedures were initiated and inspectors appointed. Yet little was accomplished, and more of the complaints about meat shortages in the latter part of the century were related to Indian consumption.[58]

The provisioning system hardened with the creation of *alhóndigas*, *pósitos*, and *abastos*. They represented the extremes to which colonial officials would go to solve problems of food distribution. How this regulation affected the nutritional consequences of conquest will probably always be a subject of speculation. Intent and result were seldom the same. Much depended on the behavior of individuals and on their commitment to fulfilling their responsibilities. Impressions from sixteenth-century records imply continual problems resulting from the chaos of conquest, overly ambitious regulations, and inadequate financing and support of local officials. Yet the records also suggest that the two major cities of the empire escaped severe, generalized shortages of food. The few bad times did not mean a century of hunger and malnutrition. This is consistent with the evidence presented elsewhere on adequate food supplies.

Determining the precise relationship between food institutions and food supply is another matter. So many economic and environmental forces affected the production and distribution of food that the political ones should not be overemphasized. Food institutions did not guarantee an adequate diet for all, but they did vocally and visibly attempt to control the distribution of food. By the end of the sixteenth century, they served as powerful intermediaries between urban needs and rural resources. As cities grew and their provisioning needs increased, their dependence on the countryside became critical. No longer did the gardens in the city, the common lands, and the many independent competing producers guarantee survival. A bad harvest or an epidemic might cause the urban population to recognize the precariousness of its situation. More frequently, hoarding and speculation—a specialty of urban food handlers just as of rural producers—hastened the calls for regulation. Food institutions and policies gave cities more control over their own destiny. They also fulfilled expectations of the way ideal communities should be organized. Just as certain social conventions were followed in the colonies, certain political institutions were seen as traditional and necessary. Food institutions fit this pattern.

5

Countervailing Forces

Descriptions of the political structure of food supplies reveal little about the diets of Indians and how they changed during the first century of colonization. Well-supplied urban centers, their nutritional needs at least recognized if not protected by policies and institutions, served Europeans first. Urban Indians might benefit, but the rural multitude lacked the protection of the city. To prove that most Indians ate well or poorly is beyond the scope of this essay. There is simply not enough evidence to quantify the diets according to modern nutritional knowledge. It is possible, however, to discuss the forces affecting diets. This provides the background necessary for evaluating specific references to the type and amount of food eaten.

Conquest threatened Indians on many fronts. One witness spoke metaphorically about the many "plagues" that harmed Indians. He meant not only disease but also public officials, merchants, private citizens, and clergy, all those who, like so many "hungry wolves among sheep," deceived and exploited Indians.[1] Of the many plagues, three had enormous potential for disrupting diets: epidemic disease and population loss; the rise of European ranching and farming; and the tribute and labor system. This chapter discusses the nutritional consequences of these intrusions on Indian life.

Population

Two incontrovertible points about the Indian population in the six-teenth century bear directly on interpretations of the food supply. First, the central areas of Mexico and the Andes supported large, settled populations. Agricultural and social adaptations had created food systems sufficient to feed large concentrations of people. Second, a sharp decline in the population began soon after the conquest; in some cases before, as disease preceded Spaniards into new areas. The most densely populated regions were hit the hardest, but few escaped the new diseases. From the Caribbean islands to the vast reaches of Mexico and Peru, smallpox, measles, typhus, influenza, and the plague all took their toll. The result was a demographic catastrophe perhaps unequalled in the history of the world.

Estimates differ widely concerning the number of Indians who perished during the great epidemics of the sixteenth century. The work of historical demographers during the last two decades has helped to clarify many issues, but the central question of the size of the Indian population in 1492 remains unanswered. For the central Andes (Peru, Bolivia, and Ecuador) and central Mexico, estimates range from 3 million to 30 million. For Hispaniola, the extremes are greater: from 100,000 to 8 million.[2] Mexican demographic history has been carefully studied, and the results have been widely cited. Cook and Borah estimate the population of central Mexico at 25.2 million in 1518. From the conquest to 1532 the population plunged to 16.8 million. The decline continued until the 1620s, when Indians numbered "approximately 730,000."[3] Andean Indians suffered the same fate. David Noble Cook demonstrates lower and upper population limits of 4 million and 14 million in 1520, and suggests a mid-range number of 9 million. By 1620 the population had declined to 600,000.[4]

Despite the controversy, the population decline proves that the absolute nutritional needs of Spanish America shrank with the conquest. Regional variation played a part as some groups recovered quickly or escaped the full impact of the epidemics. This did little to counter the unmistakable trend recognized by most contemporaries of a decline in the Indian population. There is no doubt that total food needs in 1492 were much higher than in 1600. The small Spanish population of the conquest grew quickly, creating new food demands, but these were not enough to offset the decline of Indian demand. The large, unproductive Spanish population—estimated at 4,000 to 5,000 men in Potosí alone—was frequently identified as a menace to Spaniards and Indians, but only infrequently singled out as a reason for food shortages. Apparently food supplies were adequate to support this large and troublesome group, who came "only with the capes on their backs" and who were unwilling to work.[5] Africans, brought along first as auxiliaries and servants and then as plantation slaves, probably increased food demands faster than Spaniards, but not enough to reach preconquest levels.

The overall decline in demand for food is usually not considered by historians when arguing that food shortages contributed to the population decline in the sixteenth century. Famine was an assumed cause or consequence of mortality. "Epidemics and hunger formed almost endless cycles," reducing the population and weakening the colonies.[6] In the case of Mexico at least the famines of the sixteenth century were one part of a history of hunger which periodically troubled Mexico from the fifteenth through the late eighteenth century.[7]

The evidence from the sixteenth century on famines is not persuasive. Words such as *hambre* nad *carestía* often appear in the documents, but there is little to prove that these referred to more than temporary shortages or price increases of one of the staples. When people were supposedly dying of hunger, such as the sick in Mexico City during the crisis of 1576, the impression is that the distribution of food to the sick failed, not the production of food.[8] I have not seen the evidence to prove that the sixteenth-century *hambre* was " a shortage of total food so extreme and protracted as to result in widespread persisting hunger, notable emaciation in many of the affected population, and a considerable elevation of community death rate [*sic*] attributable at least in part to death from starvation."[9] People got hungry in the sixteenth century, and probably some died of hunger, but I do not think famine was a generalized condition among Indians or Spaniards in Spanish America.[10]

Exactly how population loss influenced food supplies is not clear for all areas. The relationship between people and land was complex, with many forces influencing the production and distribution of nutrients. Cook and Borah's preliminary assessment of the situation in Mexico is a good introduction to the potential for nutritional change after the conquest. As the absolute demand for food declined, land available for agriculture increased. The crowded highland valleys of Mexico and Peru lost the most people, which freed new land for agricultural activities. As pressure on the land declined, marginal lands reverted to a natural state, while cultivation of good lands intensified, giving increased yields per unit of labor. Wages increased because of worker scarcity, and the nutritional state of Indians improved.[11] The situation was similar to the European experience after the Black Death, about which Braudel wrote that "real salaries have never been as high as they were then."[12]

In the short run, there were agricultural reversals with shortages, or at least increased prices, of basic commodities. Their population weakened by disease, fewer Indians planted and harvested. This led to increased competition for grains. Yet production seemed to rebound quickly, even after the most severe epidemics. Less than three years after the epidemic of 1589, the viceroy of Peru reported "abundant wheat," with food supplies increasing daily.[13] Midway through the crisis years of 1576–81 in Mexico, the viceroy wrote about good harvests of maize and wheat. Ten years later, Mexico was "full of provisions," even though "Indian villages continue to be stung by disease, and it seems that it has become customary that many Indians die every year."[14] Disease, "which never lacked among Indians," did not necessarily mean a shortage of food.[15] Resiliency more than anything else characterized New World agriculture by the end of the century.

Indian agricultural productivity was related to many factors. For example, there may have been a decline in the amount of time required to travel back and forth between home and agricultural plots. (Village workers in mid-twentieth-century Mexico often spent four to six hours each day traveling to their hillside plots.[16]) If late-fifteenth-century populations were as dense as many suggest, travel probably occupied an important part of the worker's day as new lands were brought under cultivation. The conquest would have reversed this situation, reducing the time needed for travel and increasing the time available for agricultural work and other activities.

Changes in family size might also have eased the pressure on available resources. Population pyramids are very difficult to construct for the sixteenth century, but it is possible to speculate that as families were reduced in size, the number of very old and very young people declined faster than the rest. In other words, the cruel streamlining effect of epidemics left populations with smaller dependent groups. If this did occur, the nutritional needs of groups struck by disease would have declined as their ability to provide for their needs declined. As populations recovered, dependent groups would once again have had to be fed from the labor of the economically active.[17]

As a result of the population decline, fewer people had more land for food production. Agriculture on the best lands produced the crop yields that so amazed Europeans. Some lands previously worked now lay fallow, replenishing their nutrients. When these lands were once again brought under cultivation, they too must have had high yields. Until that time, their natural state aided the increase of flora and fauna, which permitted hunting and gathering activities to contribute more nutrients to the diet. Small populations can usually take advantage of a wider range of foods than large, densely settled populations. The continued importance of hunting to the diet through the colonial period is understandable only within this context. After the conquest, the land had to support a much smaller human population. How well it did so depended on the intrusion of new agricultural and labor demands.

The Agricultural Impact

The rise of European ranching and farming had the potential to weaken Indian diets. Enough witnesses cried out against the despoliation of Indian maize lands to prove that this did occur in densely populated regions. When coupled with labor demands, the new agriculture could further diminish Indian diets. Carl Sauer described how changes in social organization coincided with biological changes to disrupt Indian food supplies in the Caribbean. The "delicate ecological balance broke down" as Indians were restricted to a diet of cassava, no longer having the chance to fish and hunt for protein. The carbohydrate diet provided sufficient calories, but few other nutrients. Indians did not yet eat Spanish livestock, so the result was malnutrition.[18]

On the mainland, changing land-use patterns were such a threat to Indians that the crown and local communities established legal distances between Indian plots and cattle and sheep lands. This practice was borrowed from Spain, where the battle between farmer and rancher had been waged for centuries.[19] The laws had little effect, and livestock continued their rampage, leaving hunger behind. Indeed, there appeared to be a causal relationship between the rise of cattle and the decline of the Indian population. Cattle contributed to the decline by depriving Indians of traditional staples. And as Indians died or left, more land was opened for cattle grazing.[20]

The biological and economic dynamics of colonization lessened the threat of cattle by the end of the century. As previously discussed, overgrazing and reckless slaughtering had reduced the size of herds. At the same time, an increased demand for cereals, both Indian and European, prompted the reclamation of land for crops. The result was that ranching moved to the frontier zones, where it had less effect on crops.

Interpretations of the nutritional significance of the quadruped invasion depend on what is emphasized. Images of marauder livestock destroying Indian maize plots imply a decline in nutrition. So do impressions of cattle and sheep, which are not the most efficient converters of grass to protein, displacing the more useful Andean cameloids.[21] Perhaps the agricultural self-sufficiency of some Indian communities was destroyed by European livestock.[22] It is reasonable to conclude that Indians did lose maize, although it is difficult to show how much was lost and how this contributed to malnutrition. Two observations may be of help here. First, the presence of large numbers of cattle does not automatically lead to the destruction of agriculture. India loses very little grain to the tens of millions of zebu cattle that wander freely about city and countryside. Agriculture in India is actually more productive with the cattle, which are used for power and fertilizer.[23] Second, maize prices were low during the first two generations of conquest, a time when cattle and pigs apparently ran wild and Indians had little experience in protecting their fields. It was also the time of the largest Indian population, and consequently of most intense demand for maize. By the time maize prices began to climb in the 1570s, the cattle problem was less severe for Indians in the central areas. If there had been a strong correlation between maize shortages and cattle, the chronology should have been reversed.[24]

A more balanced view recognizes the addition of new food sources but concludes that Indians "lost rather than gained" from conquest.[25] I suggest carrying this view one step further for the sixteenth century. The introduction of new foods, especially animal fats and proteins, more than compensated for any loss of Indian staples. Indians were great lovers of meat, and they soon had their own slaughterhouses and butcher shops. I think that Gibson's statement for the Valley of Mexico applies to most of Spanish America: "By 1598 it could be said that the Indian taste for meat had become fixed and unalterable."[26] Cheap meat allowed most Indians to satisfy their love of meat during the sixteenth century. Even as beef became more expensive, Indians still had pigs, goats, sheep, and European fowl. In the Andes there were still massive herds (60,000 head) of cameloids in very poor communities when European livestock was not available.[27]

The effects of wheat and other food crops on Indian diets were less dramatic. Once again, the problem is twofold: How much maize land was displaced by the new crops, and to what extent did the new crops help to offset any decline in maize consumption? Once again, the answers are indirect. In the sixteenth century wheat had the most potential for changing Indian diets, since Spaniards demanded wheat wherever they went. The demand for wheat is one possible interpretation for Spaniards' claiming and overseeing the land in response to the frustration of not being able to force Indians to plant enough wheat.[28] Furthermore, wheat competed with maize in precisely those areas that held the greatest concentration of Indians. By the end of the century, the best-irrigated lands grew wheat first, then maize. Yet the market for wheat was limited by the small European population, and the amount of maize land displaced in the sixteenth century was small. Besides, some Indians ate wheat—and barley, in the Andes—along with maize, cassava, and potatoes.[29] The economic and cultural advantages of the traditional staples guaranteed their primacy over wheat, but wheat did contribute to the Indian diet. The same was true for the dozens of other food crops introduced by Europeans. The destabilization caused by wheat should not be exaggerated.

Emphasis on the disruptive effects of the new agriculture appears more convincing in the ease of the specialty crops that served the international marketplace. Sugar, cacao, vanilla, tobacco, fibers, and dyes were grown on land that could serve subsistence needs. Indians ate large amounts of some of the export foods, especially sugar and cacao, but the nutritional benefits were modest. As demand for these goods increased in Europe, more land was devoted to their production in the New World. The process began soon after conquest and continued. The point at which the export economy began to impinge on subsistence needs varied a great deal from region to region. It is possible to argue for Mexico that by 1600 sugar was a threat to subsistence production. By that time, sugar plantations had absorbed much land on a line stretching from Veracruz to Cuernavaca.[30] The argument is possible, but not convincing. Maize lands were displaced, and labor was secured, but there is little evidence of widespread hunger as a result. Two hundred years later when commercial agriculture was much more advanced, Mexico still produced mainly subsistence foods. Humboldt remarked that "even though Mexican agriculture, like all countries whose products suffice for the basic needs of the population, is directed mainly toward the production of subsistence foods, it does not mean that Mexico is less rich in what are called exclusively colonial foods."[31] Clearly, export agriculture had not yet overwhelmed subsistence agriculture. The same was true of the Spanish Caribbean, where sugar production traced its origins to the early sixteenth century. Subsistence agriculture held its own against commercial agriculture into the nineteenth century.[32]

Land availability was the essential variable. In most of Spanish America, including Cuba, enough land was available to meet both subsistence and export agricultural needs. With sufficient land, farmers did not have to agonize over whether to plow or leave fallow, plant crops or let animals graze, or grow food for home consumption or for market. Agriculture for export markets was found primarily in areas of low population density, and thus did not compete with subsistence lands. Even when commercial crops were grown in heavily populated areas, such as the coca valleys of Peru or the sugar valleys of central Mexico, it would be hard to prove that this limited subsistence production. When limited land forced hard decisions, as in the small island of Barbados after the English introduced sugarcane plantations, commercial agriculture could snuff out subsistence agriculture within a few years.[33] This was not the case for most of Spanish America, where abundant lands were still available at the end of the sixteenth century. The rapid expansion of export agriculture in the late nineteenth century came from lands that had been vacant or used for subsistence agriculture in the sixteenth century. During the first century of colonization the vastness of the land easily accommodated the new agricultural needs of Europeans as well as the old ones of Indians.

Labor and Tribute

It was widely believed in the sixteenth century that "the republic of Spaniards in no manner would survive without aid from the Indian."[34] From the first days of bartering and trading through the rise of complex systems of labor and tribute, Indians supplied nutrients to the colony.

Wherever Spaniards encountered large Indian populations, they introduced arrangements such as the *encomienda* and *repartimiento* to secure labor. *Encomienda* and *repartimiento* were variants of the same principle of Spanish dominance and Indian subordinance. Under the *encomienda*, Indians provided labor and tribute to Spaniards. Never static, the *encomienda* underwent many changes and gradually lost the rights to labor and personal services. By the end of the sixteenth century, the crown rather than private individuals exacted tribute. As the *encomienda* weakened, *repartimiento*, a form of compulsory rotational labor, directed Indians to work for

Spaniards. Other compulsory practices, some of them borrowed from the days before the conquest, helped control Indians.

Studies of labor and tribute in Mexico, Central America, and the Andes show that the new demands shook Indian life, weakening communities and leading to stronger Spanish control over the land. A "plunder economy," exacting more and more tribute and labor, ultimately condemned Indians to a life of poverty and dependence on the new masters.[35]

Mines, cities, and plantations competed for labor. Mining interests in particular relentlessly pursued their claim to labor and usually found local and imperial support for their demands. Motolinía, one of the earliest writers to describe mining on the mainland, was horrified at the widespread "stench" of death surrounding the mines where so many "dead bodies or bones" covered the roads. Indians were forced to bring their own food to the mines, and died if they did not.[36] In Potosí, after the high profits of the early years, the conditions of workers became more difficult. The *mita* labor draft instituted by Francisco de Toledo in 1573 forced Indians into the mines, where hard work and scarce food made life difficult. They often had to travel to the mines bringing their own food, which spoiled on the way. High prices and inadequate wages faced them in the mining camps, limiting food consumption. Just as bad were the danger of working with mercury and the lack of adequate clothing.[37]

The squeeze between wages and prices for mine workers became tighter toward the end of the century, forcing more careful use of resources. Whether hunger resulted as a widespread, ongoing problem is still not known. An interesting piece of evidence is the response to the very damaging report of Juan Ortiz de Zárate, *corregidor* of Potosí, who had listed the many ways Indians were abused. Witnesses responded to many of the charges, but there was little discussion of food shortages or hunger. Apparently food was not an issue in the welfare of miners. As for the general abuse of workers, one witness put it well: "Some miners treat Indians well, others badly."[38]

Most Indians were not completely dependent on their employers. Laws required that workers receive food and clothing at fair prices; new *albóndigas* supposedly guaranteed grain supplies; mining codes fixed rations of maize, chiles, and beans; wage scales took into account the food costs of Indians.[39] One ardent supporter of forced labor in Mexico went so far as to argue that since Indians received hot meat and maize as laborers instead of just one cold tamale they should be forced to work for longer periods.[40] It would be hasty to dismiss the laws passed for the welfare of Indian as only another example of the rhetoric of the colonial mind. The intent of the legislation was taken seriously. To assist production, the state recognized the need to control—or at least influence—consumption, ensuring that Indians would eat well enough to be active in the labor force.[41] The call for meat in the diet of mine workers was one recognition of the relationship between labor productivity and nutrition. Chevalier, referring to contemporary sources, said that "only a meat diet could sustain the hard work" of mining.[42] Small, isolated mines also had enough livestock to recommend meat for the diet.[43]

Despite the economic importance of mining, it represented a very small part of the labor burden Indians carried. In the late sixteenth century, Mexico and Potosí each had between 9,000 and 10,000 mine workers, and most of these were voluntary rather than forced workers. [44] What is known about the wages of forced workers, which were reduced by tribute demands, indicates that they were inadequate for support.[45] The question then becomes one of alternative sources of food and income, particularly the role of rations and how these contributed to nutritional well-being. More perplexing is the question of why Indians voluntarily kept coming to the mines, risking their health and freedom, if many workers were starving. At this point, it is not possible to prove that Indian miners were malnourished. Even if it could be proved, it would tell us little about Indian workers in general. Given the special geographic problems of mining camps and the high price of food, it would be a mistake to assume that living conditions there applied to other areas.

Most Indians toiled in fields and factories, built houses and cathedrals, and worked on irrigation and drainage projects. Indian labor destroyed the old and built the new. The scope of the new was monumental and apparently came about only through increasing demands on Indians. There is much to support this view.[46] But much evidence, coming from Indians and Spaniards, suggests that the labor demands of the early colony were less than those of the pre-conquest years. Time and again Indians in the Andes and Mexico said they worked less under the Spaniards than in the past, although this was not always beneficial to Indians. George Kubler explains the situation by emphasizing the ritual significance of labor among Indians before the conquest, and showing how the culture of the Indian suffered under the new concepts of work.[47]

A question remains about the amount of work expected and received from Indians in the sixteenth century. There were so many complaints about the difficulties of forcing Indians to work that it is tempting to see some validity in them. "By their nature Indians were enemies of work, and fled whenever they had the chance." The Inca had supposedly solved the problem by giant make-work programs, forcing Indians "to move mountains" to keep them strong and occupied.[48] If they worked at all, it was only after much coercion.[49] Indians were lazier than in the past, but at the same time they were eating and drinking more.[50] In the case of Quito, food, which "costs them almost nothing," was specifically mentioned as a cause of Indian vagabondage.[51]

These views reflected deep prejudices that grew out of the early years of conquest. They also served as justifications for trying to exercise even greater control over Indians. The end result was not always what Spaniards anticipated. Control over labor remained a problem. The evidence implies that abundant food supplies made it more difficult for Spaniards to force Indians to work.

After the first years of conquest, much of the labor, both free and forced, was wage labor. In central Mexico, workers experienced substantial wage increases through the century. To take the example of unskilled day laborers, wages increased from one-fourth of a real in the 1540s to three-fourths of a real in the 1570s, rising to one and one-half reals by 1603.[52] Maize prices also rose during the century, building on the plateaus reached after the major epidemics of 1545–48 and 1576–81. After 1579, prices seldom fell below ten reals a *fanega*, and never dropped to the one- and two-real prices seen before the 1550s.[53]

The precise relationship between wages, prices, and diets is a complex problem. Borah and Cook state that "in 1590 the daily money wage of an unskilled workman bought approximately three times as much corn as a day's wage in 1530, despite the rise in the price of corn."[54] Evidence from provincial towns also suggests that Indians had the purchasing power to buy abundant quantities of mutton and grain.[55] In addition, it should be noted that Indian wages at times included rations. Enough examples of rations exist to prove that food payments in addition to specie payments were not unusual. Indians who actually received specie and food payments, even the poorly paid *repartimiento* worker, had the potential for a good diet.

The problem with this reasoning is that Indians had multiple obligations under their new masters. They also had to pay tribute, at times in specie, at times in deliveries of food and fiber. Circumstances and amounts varied, but tribute was a method of political and economic control familiar to both Spaniards and Indians. After the conquest, Spain continued and perhaps increased the old tribute demands. From the first years of the sixteenth century, Indians gave maize, wheat, eggs, chickens, fruits, fish, and cloth to Europeans. Complex provisioning systems emerged, as Indians villages were assigned goods to deliver to urban markets. As an additional burden, they faced artificially imposed low prices that limited their profits.[56]

Spaniards doggedly pursued tribute through the centuries. Charles Gibson, whose study of the Aztecs is still one of the best discussions of tribute, describes the complexity of tribute: its different forms, the way it changed through time, and the determination to collect tribute, even if this meant jailing the descendants of those who did not pay. Whether in Middle America or the Andes, tribute was an incessant burden for Indians, often falling more heavily on the community than the individual and limiting the ability of Indians to enjoy the products of their own labor. Tribute, when combined with other taxes and labor obligations, began to break down Indian communities.[57]

Tribute and labor policies imposed heavy burdens on the Spanish American provisioning system. Just as importantly, they disrupted Indian life, especially during the chaotic years of conquest and settlement. The many *memorias* for the good treatment of the Indians make clear that the Spanish presence strained the Indian food supply. Indians who had to carry food to cities and mines and to work in Spanish houses and fields had less time for their own agricultural pursuits. As they were forced to produce and exchange Spanish food, their own diets changed and became less diverse. Disruptions in Indian market practices, as Europeans commandeered Indian goods and changed market schedules to suit their own needs, also influenced food supply.[58]

Tribute was the most durable and institutionalized of the many demands placed on Indians. There is no doubt that it both reduced Indian purchasing power, as it had before the conquest, and limited consumption. During periods of food shortages, the tribute burden probably increased hunger for many. Exactly where and how often this occurred is difficult to say. Contemporaries held conflicting opinions on the appropriateness of tribute. A 1554 report in Mexico, commenting on whether tribute was heavier then than before the conquest, and whether it should be continued, responded that "there is very great confusion on this point."[59] The effects on Indian life were not immediately and uniformly disastrous. Recent scholarship on Andean Indians suggests that some communities withstood the many threats of conquest remarkably well, displaying "an internal vitality that enabled them to survive—for a time—as relatively autonomous and modestly prosperous productive units."[60]

Tribute had other implications for the food supply. Beginning in the early 1550s in Mexico, royal edicts reduced the obligation of Indians to deliver tribute to urban areas, leading to an increase in prices. More serious was the permission to pay tribute in specie rather than in kind. As the multiple obligations of Indians were changed to money payments, there was a decline in production, or at least contemporaries complained constantly of a decline. Just as the elimination of personal service had led to an increase in the price of labor, changes in tribute requirements led to an increase in the price of food. In both Mexico and Peru, Indians neglected their fields and flocks since they no longer had to deliver food. The crown attorney in Lima noted that before the commutation decrees, Indians had to work to pay their tribute. "Now with only a modest effort and little time they earn enough money to pay their tribute."[61] Apparently, with the increased silver in circulation, it was much easier to pay in silver than in food. In a curious way, tribute had actually come to be blamed for the increasing price of grain in the cities. The response was to force Indians to plant land in maize or wheat, and to try to limit payment of food tribute in specie.[62]

There was little that was inevitable about the nutritional outcome of the conquest as Europeans and Indians worked out their dietary needs. Conquest and the attempted subordination of the Indian population did not automatically create impoverished nutritional regimes. Despite the demands of labor and tribute, enough food was available, some of it the direct result of the intrusions, for Indians to improve their diets.

6

Indian Food and Drink

It is easier to discuss the forces that influenced Indian diets than to describe the diets themselves. Evidence of what and how much Indians actually ate is scarce. Scattered references have to be patched together to present a general description of dietary change. Assumptions about diet influence the way the evidence is presented and interpreted.

Just as an assumed causal relationship between conquest and a decline in Indian nutrition can be misleading, so can other assumptions, particularly those based on belief in the continuity of Indian diets. Poor Indian diets today do not necessarily mean poor diets in the sixteenth century. Nor do the changes experienced by twentieth-century Indians as they come into contact with new nutritional regimes always provide answers to questions of dietary change in the past. Similarly, Indian agricultural and food systems of the fifteenth century do not automatically apply to the sixteenth century. The recent discovery of sophisticated land-use systems in the society of the pre-conquest Maya and the possible role of ramón (breadnut tree) as a staple comparable in importance to maize are examples of challenges to traditional beliefs about pre-Columbian food and agriculture.[1] So little is known about food use in Latin America that it is risky to borrow information from one period to explain another.

Food habits are often assumed to be stable parts of culture, rigid and resistant to change. Changes in food habits announce broader social changes and suggest deep cultural transformations.[2] Given the complex relationship between culture and diet, it is difficult to verify this for the sixteenth century. It can be shown, however, that Indians accepted many new foods and still remained "Indian" within the context of the sixteenth century. Diets did change as a result of the conquest, and at times they appeared to do so much faster than other parts of culture. The evidence leaves us far short of unassailable conclusions about the extent and quality of the change, but it does reinforce the hypothesis that food supplies werre adequate for most of the century.

Indian Foods

Any sketch of Indian nutritional regimes has to emphasize the staples. They stand out like large mountains on the horizon, overshadowing the foothills that surround them. The Caribbean and coastal lowlands relied on cassava, known as *yuca* in much of Spanish America and *mandioca* in Brazil. *Yuca brava*, a tuber containing potentially toxic amounts of cyanide, was widely consumed. With the cyanide expressed, it was usually processed as flour and served as gruel and bread. Maize, so versatile and productive, similarly dominated the diet of Mexico, Central America, and the lower elevations of the Andes. In the altiplano the potato, a hardy tuber capable of being freeze dried and preserved as *chuño*, was the staple. As the dominant sources of carboyhydrates, these foods had nutritional and perhaps cultural roles similar to that of rice in China, wheat in the Mediterranean, and taro in the Pacific islands.[3]

Maize was an especially versatile food. The Aztec lords of the land ate maize as exquisitely prepared tortillas. Some were large, thick, and white; others small, delicate, and colored. Steamed under a hot cloth or warmed on stones, they were served open or folded. Filled with fish or fowl, flavored with chiles and herbs, the versatility of the tortilla equaled that of any bread that civilization has produced. Maize was also the basis for many gruels and porridges, some carefully seasoned and sweetened, others nutritious despite their simplicity.[4] Andean Indians were no less creative. They ate maize toasted as *cancha*, cooked or popped as *mote*, and festively mixed with eggs, sugar, and spices, and served as *mazamorra*.[5] When a social history of maize and its uses is written, it will tell us much about changes in Latin American culture.

Charles Gibson's pithy summation of Indian diets in Central Mexico confirms the centrality of maize. "The truth is that Indians ate well when maize was plentiful and starved when maize was scarce."[6] Murdo MacLeod's suggestion that maize made up 90 percent of Indian diets in Central America supports the contention.[7] The diets of modern Indians, who at times rely on maize for up to 70 percent of their calories, further document the essential role of maize.[8]

These estimates may be too high for the sixteenth century. If maize or other staples had constituted such a large percentage of the Indian diet in the past, nutritional well-being would have been threatened in two obvious ways. First, nutritional deficiency diseases would have been inescapable. Maize, potatoes, and cassava provided necessary carbohydrates and calories, but did not provide sufficient amounts of other nutrients. Thiamine, riboflavin, and niacin would have headed a long list of deficient nutrients that would have weakened defenses against disease. Diseases such as pellagra, the dreaded scourge of the maize cultures of the southeastern United States and the Mediterranean, and kwashiorkor, a severe form of protein deficiency, would have weakened generation after generation. Second, such heavy reliance on one food would have rendered the population particularly vulnerable to changes in supply of the staple. Pests, fungi, frosts, and droughts can attack one food more than another. When the staple does not produce, famine follows.

The emphasis on maize, cassava, and potatoes in the diet is not misplaced; it simply needs balance. Descriptions of Indians as healthy and strong challenge the idea of monotonous, single-food diets. Columbus described the first men whom he saw as "very well built, of very handsome bodies and very fine faces . . . They are generally fairly tall and good looking, well built." Later he said, "The legs of all, without exception, are very straight and [they have] no paunch, but are very well proportioned."[9] Early impressions of Indians might have been distorted, but there is little doubt that the Caribbean, Mesoamerica, and the Central Andes were complex, rich ecosystems producing foods sufficient for sustaining population increases.

In the Caribbean, maize, along with fruits, fish, and small land animals, supplemented cassava. In Mexico, maize was still referred to in the eighteenth century as "a sacred thing," indispensable to perceptions of an adequate diet.[10] It was not, however, indispensable to full bellies and nutritional well-being. Different types of beans, pumpkins, squashes, jícamas, and *camotes* provided nutrients. Amaranth, a high-protein grain, and *chía (Salvia hispanica)*, yielding nutritious seeds, were widely consumed. Magueys, tunas, tomatoes, *jitomates*, chiles, pineapples, papayas, guavas, avocados and many other fruits and vegetables contributed nutrients. Before the conquest, Mexicans cultivated some eighty different plants, and most of these provided food.[11]

Many of the foods soon had their own reputations. The belief that chile "awakens the appetite and helps digestion" was common by the end of the century.[12] Avocados, with their high oil content and rich nutty flavor, had special importance in the diet of the poor.[13] So did jícama, whose easy preservation and nutritional quality was increasingly recognized by Spaniards in the eighteenth century.[14] Cacao made a drink so nutritious that "one can go the whole day after taking a cup in the morning."[15] Maguey was one of the most versatile plants. Medical texts by the 1560s reported that "no other tree in the world had so many properties and virtues." All Indians grew maguey around their houses, and made wine, oil, vinegar, and honey from it. If necessary, they could also eat its leaves.[16] Fishing, hunting, and gathering added more nutrients to the diet. All lessened the vulnerability of the population to nutritional diseases.

In the Andes, *oca, ullucu*, and *mashua* were other types of tubers produced alongside potatoes. Quinoa and *cañihua*, grains containing large amounts of protein, complemented the starchy tubers. "Delicious and sustaining" stews were made from the small seeds.[17] From the lower elevations highland peoples traded for maize, peppers, tunas, *chirimoyas*, and passionflowers, to say nothing of berries, nuts, and seeds. In addition, Andean peoples counted on cameloids and small domesticated animals for proteins and fats.

Indians were also marvelously thorough in tapping the varied food resources of their environment.[18] Motolinía saw this in the 1530s, and commented that Indians could "endure barren years better and more easily than other races," because of eating roots and herbs.[19] These were akin to the many roots, seeds, nuts, and fruits that the Maya had classified as "famine foods."[20] By the eighteenth century, writers exaggerated that New World peoples would never starve because they ate anything and everything, an exaggeration that had a good deal of truth in it.[21]

Nutritionists can carry the argument further. "The stature [*talla elevada*] of the Aztecs, their robust complexion, their bellicose and expanionist nature can be explained by their use of mixed food regimes with extraordinarily rich proteins."[22] This is pushing nutritional determinism a little too far, but it does illustrate an important point. *Jumiles, axayácatles,* and *ahuahutles*—the insects, flies, and larvae eaten in the central valley—contained large amounts of amino acids, vitamins, and minerals. Some contributed astonishingly to the diet. Modern analyses of the tiny dried fish *charales* show that they contain about 75 grams of protein in every 100 grams, plus abundant quantities of phosphorus, calcium, and iron.[23] Social distinctions that are not yet entirely understood governed the use of these foods, as they did of tortillas and meats.[24]

It is possible to shift the emphasis from the protein content of these foods to the inefficiency of using them as primary sources of protein. Protein scarcity forced the Aztecs to the time consuming tasks of grubbing for worms and collecting tiny fish and algae from lakes. It is in this context that protein shortages have enlivened the debate over Aztec cannabilism. It is probably incorrect to argue that protein shortages caused cannabilism, but it is understandable that victims of warfare and sacrifice might end up in the pot.[25]

Foods introduced by Europeans soon accompanied traditional Indian foods. Grains, animal foods, and bananas have already been mentioned as new additions to the diets.[26] The consumption of beef gave Indians a diet superior to that prevailing in Europe in the sixteenth century. Specialty foods had the same effect. Sugar, which did not become a part of workers' diets in Europe until the nineteenth century, was widely consumed by Indians in the sixteenth century.[27] Each new food contributed nutrients, helping to create complex and varied nutritional regimes. Indians who maintained control over their nutritional destiny chose from a variety of different foods, escaping dependency on just one food.

Rations

For Indians incorporated into Spanish labor systems, evidence exists concerning the quantity of food consumed. These Indians probably had less access to hunting and gathering, but they did not lack adequate quantities of food, at least in comparison to what is known about European diets in the sixteenth century. Many Indians, as part of their labor agreement, received food rations. Meat was so abundant that it was often included as a part of rations. Mine workers in the Caribbean expected one pound of meat a day, even on fast days. The viceroy in Mexico recommended one *cuartillo* of maize and one pound of meat a day for Indian workers. Indians in textile shops in Querétaro claimed that they received meat a couple of times a day. There was talk in Mexico City that Indians, accustomed to eating "light" foods, got sick from eating too much beef and mutton. In the provinces of Peru, where meat might have been more scarce than in Mexico, Indians received less, but rations still called for a minimum of one-half pound of "good meat" a day.[28] Since beef was cheap in the sixteenth century, it is tempting to conclude that prescribed meat rations were actually given, not just recommended.

Maize was a part of rations more often than meat. One of the earliest references to maize rations comes from Mexico in 1536, when Viceroy Antonio de Mendoza insisted that Indians receive at least as much as slaves, or one *cuartillo* of maize, plus chile and tortillas. This formula was repeated later in the century and may have become standard in Mexico and Peru.[29] There were calls for as much as forty-eight *cuartillos* a month (one *fanega*), especially for mine workers, but this was apparently higher than the average.[30] Recommended amounts for women were usually less than for men, as in the ordinances for the government of Lima in the 1550s, where men received eight *almudes* (thirty-two *cuartillos*) each month, and women one-half *fanega* (twenty-four *cuartillos*).[31]

Calculations of the caloric value of the *cuartillo* range from approximately 3,350 calories to 3,800 calories.[32] Cook and Borah, who support the smaller estimate, think this amount was intended for a man and his wife. This would reduce the individual ration for an adult male to between 1,120 calories and 1,676 calories.[33] This was not a subsistence ration, but compared to the 2,000 calories Europeans supposedly consumed it was a substantial amount.[34] A few supplements, such as *sabadijos*, a couple of ounces of beans, beef, pork fat, or sugar, or an egg, would push the diet to or beyond 2,000 calories.

Other questions arise in addition to those of the size and nutritional value of rations: Were rations actually given? How many people depended on the rations? How were rations distributed within the family? What foods supplemented the rations? These questions are impossible to answer for the sixteenth century. This does not completely invalidate the use of rations for historical interpretation. Rations reflected contemporary assessments of the availability of foodstuffs and beliefs about the nutritional needs of different groups. Although they were not always given, they were usually consistent with the subsistence realities of a time and place. Gradually they came to represent more than food. They represented a reciprocal social and biological relationship essential to colonial society, which helped to bind individuals and groups. Teachers, orphans, apprentices, priests, nuns, beggars, and others, in addition to Indians, lived from rations.[35] My impression after reviewing ration recommendations from different time periods is that they support the idea of adequate food supplies.

One of the difficulties arising from this impression is that ration recommendations exceeded some of the popular stereotypes of how much Indians ate. According to one view, Indians, regardless of habitat and economy, ate only enough food for subsistence, ignoring the sensuous pleasures associated with food that were so dear to Europeans. The many condiments, spices, and elaborate preparations essential to European culture failed to interest Indians, who were content to eat grains and tubers seasoned with a dash of pepper or cassava juice. Motolinía thought Indian food "extremely poor and scanty."[36] Books with just a passing reference to the New World found Indian eating habits so distinctive that they commented on them. Christóbal Méndez in his *Book of Bodily Exercises* (1553) described how the Indians traveled with a little maize, an herb with salt, maybe a lizard or worm, and some chile.[37] Officials complained about Indian workers who had no interest in the future and survived on a little toasted maize and water.[38] Later Clavijero noted how earlier writers talked about "the wonder to see the Spaniards eat more in one day than they [Indians] did in a week."[39] Perhaps Cañete y Domínguez was right when he said that Indians in Potosí ate about one-half as much as Spaniards ate.[40]

Hunters and gatherers had a different reputation. According to eighteenth-century accounts, some remarkable eaters consumed eight to ten pounds of meat in one sitting. Indians apparently had the capacity to adjust to the availability of foods with enviable ease. They gorged themselves when they could, but lived quite satisfactorily when food was scarce.[41] Such practices were seldom a part of the central areas. Sedentary agricultural societies had regular food supplies that permitted the development of eating customs more consistent with European expectations.

The view of Indians as "small feeders" becomes more interesting when placed in the context of the sixteenth century. Popular perceptions held that Indian diets, or rather the quantity of food consumed, increased after the conquest. Under the Inca, Indians "ate and drank less than now."[42] To their traditional diets of grains, tubers, fruits, and vegetables, Indians added beef, pork, fowl, and many other foods. Throughout central Mexico, most Indians reported that they ate less before the conquest than in the early 1580s. They made these statements after the most severe epidemic affecting the Mexican population (1576–81).[43] The result was not necessarily a better nutritional regime, as new and more abundant foods could lead to poor health. "And they said that they were stronger and lived longer before, even though they worked more and ate less."[44] The moderation and temperance of pre-conquest eating habits gave way to excessive or improper eating, which in turn led to population loss.

Cook and Borah have already recognized that Indians' food consumption increased after conquest.[45] Borah has further refined their conclusions, suggesting that Indians consumed on average from 1,700 to 2,000 calories a day. Since so many different foods were available, this should be the low range. Meat and lard might have been more available to the poor than Cook and Borah suggest, which would push actual consumption of calories much higher.[46]

The best conclusion that can be drawn from the conflicting evidence is that Indians probably did eat less than Spaniards, despite the increase in consumption after the conquest. The implications of this are not clear. If the idea of an abundant Spanish diet is accepted, then the fact that Indians ate less than Spaniards does not mean their diets were inadequate. There is still no compelling evidence for long-term malnutrition, or even undernourishment, in the sixteenth century. Indians ate less than Spaniards in the New World, but not less than Europeans at home. The reason is that diets were diverse. The combination of New World and Old World foods in addition to the readiness of Indians to enjoy what Europeans found repugnant enriched and diversified the diet. Mice, snakes, lizards, worms, caterpillars, along with countless other small crawling and flying things, were welcomed on the plate along with grains and meats.

Drink as Food

Indian eating had much to do with Indian drinking. Indians, along with Europeans, consumed enormous quantities of alcoholic beverages, which in turn influenced the food they needed and consumed. Of the many beverages common to the sixteenth century, *chicha* and pulque had the most influence on local life. *Chicha* was a fermented drink made from grains or fruits found throughout Spanish America but most popular in the Andes. *Pulque* was the fermented sap of the agave plant and was widely consumed in Mexico. Both have a very long history, and both remain a part of Indian life today.

Three interrelated hypotheses on Indian drinking help to explain the history of food and colonization. First, the supply of alcoholic beverages increased in the sixteenth century, far surpassing availability in the fifteenth century. Second, this led to, or at least permitted, increased consumption, which once again exceeded that of the fifteenth century. Third, the beverages supplied valuable nutrients, which limited the consumption of other foods.

The changing relationship between food production and population size influenced the supply of *chicha* and pulque. During the last years of the Inca and Aztec empires, population pressures limited the use of arable land to the production of staples for consumption. The legal and social sanctions against drinking were reinforced by ecological considerations. And control over alcoholic beverages was easier to maintain when most of the land was used for the production of staples. The ritual use of *chicha* and pulque is easily understood within this context. A narrowly defined use of alcohol was consistent with a limited supply.

As pressure on the land decreased, the production of *chicha* and pulque increased, or at least per capita production increased. The introduction of Spanish wine, beer, grape brandy, and cane brandy also contributed to the growing per capita supply of alcoholic beverages. Vineyards in the hot valleys of Peru and Chile produced hundreds of thousands of *botijas* (19 to 23 gallons) of wine by the end of the century. As a result, prices started to fall in some of the valleys.[47] Indians and blacks were drinking this wine in the taverns of Lima by the late 1540s.[48] Later in the colonial period cane brandy made great inroads. In eighteenth-century Quito, Indians could drink sixteen times as much cane brandy as grape brandy for the same price.[49]

The use of coca paralleled that of alcohol. Before the conquest, limited coca supplies resulted in more frequent use by nobles than commoners.[50] After the conquest, coca quickly became a prominent feature of the new order. It was most evident in the mining camps, where Indians who used coca could supposedly "work all day without eating."[51] Land availability and weakened sanctions against usage promoted the widespread usage of coca.

For urban people, access to *chicha*, pulque, and other beverages required effective distribution. All of the evidence points to the emergence of a retail system adequate to the task. *Pulperías, pulquerías*, and *chicherías* were common in most towns. Mexico City had 30 taverns selling to Indians by 1540; Lima had 20 by 1550. By the end of the colonial period, Mexico City had some 1,600 taverns, literally one on every street corner.[52] The politics of regulating these taverns began in the 1540s and continued through the colonial period.

Demand for *chicha* and pulque was satisfied more readily in the sixteenth than the fifteenth century. Under the Aztecs, drunkenness was supposedly roundly condemned and severely punished. Under the Inca, the use of *chicha* hinged on reciprocal political arrangements. In both cultures, drinking was carefully regulated, so that ritual drinking blended with the political need to maintain control.[53] Of course there is no way to determine how much was actually consumed in the fifteenth or sixteenth century, but the evidence implies an increase in consumption. The "main reason for their short lives is too much drinking, a privilege of caciques in the past" was a typical comment of the sixteenth century. Officials constantly complained about drunk Indians, who were incapable of working.[54] There are too many comments of this sort to discount them.[55]

How much consumption was "too much"? For all the rhetoric, few bothered to note specific amounts. Speculative calculations can be made. Potosí used 50,000 *fanegas* of maize flour to produce 1.6 million *botijas* of *chicha* in 1603. With an estimated Indian population of 60,000, of whom perhaps 50 percent regularly drank *chicha*, per capita yearly consumption was 53 *botijas*, or about 3 gallons a day.[56] Not the least of the difficulties with this type of figuring is that Potosí was an exceptional city with exceptional lifestyles. Its reputation as the *chicha* capital of the Andes was confirmed by Cañete y Domínguez in the eighteenth century when he described the "incredible and infinite" number of *pulperías* and *chicherías* selling *chicha* and brandy.[57] Substantial drinking also continued in Mexico. The drinking population of Mexico City consumed about two liters per capita per day.[58] Changes through the centuries are hard to document, but it is known that residents of the capital in 1939 still drank about two liters a day.[59] Essentially the same was true for rural Otomi Indians in the 1940s, who were known to drink as much as 10 liters a day.[60]

Whether Indian drinking was excessive depends on the point of view. The European drinking experience was complex, and Spaniards were perhaps the most abstemious of western Europeans. Few sixteenth-century observers should have been alarmed at the amount of Indian drinking. Ration records indicate substantial daily consumption by Europeans. English sailors and servants drank up to one gallon of beer a day; Dutch sailors drank as much as two gallons a day; Spanish sailors preferred wine, about one liter a day when they could get it.[61] Overall, European drinking was on the increase in the sixteenth century, and continued to rise in the seventeenth and eighteenth centuries.[62] Impressions of Indian drinking were nurtured within this context of what was normal consumption.

Alarm over *chicha* and pulque perhaps had less to do with amounts consumed than with associated practices. Bishop Zumárraga wished to outlaw pulque in 1529 because it smacked of idolatry. The missionary advance was just beginning, and drinking, with its ritual vestiges, was a major obstacle.[63] There were also material concerns. The first brewery for European-style beer was established in Mexico in 1544. The crown, recognizing that the brewery could not survive without some protection, forbade Spaniards or Indians to make or sell local beverages.[64]

Many of the sixteenth-century laws aimed at eliminating specific religious and economic problems, not at controlling widespread drinking. This is consistent with William Taylor's conclusion that ritual drinking continued to regulate pulque consumption. Taylor believes that increases in consumption were less dramatic than assumed, and that they lacked deeply disruptive effects.[65] There is little doubt that pulque and *chicha* maintained their ritual status. Used during planting, harvesting, and community activities to invoke divine intervention, they strengthened the social bonds of Indian life. *Chicha* in modern Peru, for example, has an alimentary function as a drink and as a food; in addition, it has social, economic, religious, and medical functions, all vital to the existence of the community.[66]

The ritual importance of *chicha* and pulque is not inconsistent with increased consumption. Certainly many Indians consumed substantial amounts of pulque and *chicha*, and at times this was socially disruptive. Small, stable agricultural communities like Querétaro and large tumultuous cities like Potosí suffered from unruly Indian drinking by the end of the sixteenth century.[67]

Charles Gibson chose to end his monumental study of the Aztecs by emphasizing the role of alcohol in the clash of the two cultures. "One of the earliest and most persistent individual responses was drink. If our sources may be believed, few peoples in the whole of history were more prone to drunkeness than the Indians of the Spanish colony."[68] Theories of alcoholism offer an explanation. Alcohol as a social phenomenon helps to ease tensions and anxieties caused by threats to the social order.[69] When groups and institutions which have previously provided stability are weakened or destroyed, excessive use of alcohol may follow.[70] Sixteenth-century Spanish America seems to support the theories. Fundamental, far-reaching forces shook the Aztec and Inca worlds in the sixteenth century. By 1600, much of the past was only a vague memory, recaptured in ceremonies that were increasingly influenced by Europeans. The collapse of empires and subjugation by invaders led to an increased reliance on alcohol as a means of escape from the stress of a rapidly changing world. Institutions that had previously guaranteed stability and continuity began to weaken. Family life, community political organization, and religious ways all suffered as populations collapsed and the invaders introduced new patterns of work and settlement. The result was drunkenness.

The genetic argument offers another explanation. Since the conquest, Indians have frequently been depicted as particularly vulnerable to alcohol. One of the first serious attempts to study Indian drunkenness was based on the premise that Indians had "an innate and inborn inclination toward alcoholic beverages."[71] Some recent studies emphasize the different rates at which alcohol is metabolized by Indians and Caucasians, arguing that "Indians metabolize alcohol at a significantly slower rate than the whites."[72] The issue is far from resolved, and is part of the ongoing nature-nurture debate.

Several other reasons can be mentioned. Observers thought pulque gave warmth, made a good substitute for polluted water, and had medicinal properties.[73] And the matter of taste should not be ignored. Individually and collectively Indians enjoyed the taste of pulque and *chicha*. The beverages satisfied a physiological need, and at the same time fulfilled widely esteemed cultural expectations. When the sanctions against frequent use weakened and the supply increased, the demand could be satisfied.

For this study, the nutritional explanation is particularly interesting. From the earliest years of conquest, the nutritional benefits of *chicha* and pulque were cited. Oviedo said that maize *chicha* was "very healthful" and that Indians used it "as a primary foodstuff."[74] Carletti, visiting Peru in the 1590s, was much impressed with the "substance and nourishment" of *chicha*, despite being appalled by the "old women with slobbering mouths" who made it.[75] Juan and Ulloa thought *chicha* contributed to the "healthy, strong, and robust" appearance of Indians around Quito.[76] Another supporter was Unanue, who claimed that "the strength and obesity of Indians who eat little but drink much *chicha* is proof that *chicha* is very nutritious.[77] Pulque did not command the same respect. Early indictments argued that additives to pulque, such as roots and lime, made the drink debilitating, though this did little to curtail consumption.[78] Two hundred years later opinions had changed. The *Diario de México*, one of the most widely read publications in Mexico City, announced that pulque was a healthful and nutritious drink if taken in moderation.[79]

Modern assessments confirm the nutritional value of *chicha* and pulque. Pulque has useful amounts of vitamins C and B[1] plus thiamin, riboflavin, niacin, calcium, iron, and the amino acids tryptophan and tyrosine. *Chicha* also contains essential vitamins and minerals in addition to calories.[80] Both are vital when the general diet is meager. They are not, however, more nutritious than many of the other foods in the Indian diet. A recent study of *chicha* in Colombia confirms *chicha's* nutritional value, but identifies it as a primary cause of illness since it reduces the appetite for and consumption of more nutritious foods. Money spent for *chicha* could be more wisely spent on other foods.[81] Despite their limitations, *chicha* and pulque did and do contribute nutrients to the Indian diet.

Here then is one possible explanation for the many comments about the spare eating of Indians: *Chicha* and pulque supplied nutrients lost by eating so little. If this is true, did Indians drink because of the lack of food, or did drinking reduce the appetite and need for other foods? In his observation on drinking and tobacco use in Europe, Fernand Braudel offers a possible answer. Peasants turned to alcohol in ever-increasing numbers as food supplies became scarce. Wine and beer became cheap foodstuffs in addition to being a *"quita-penas,"* a release from the pressures of life. In the same way, tobacco helped people cope with the anxiety and pain of food shortages.[82] The increased use of coca in the Andes would fit this interpretation. Burdened by an oppressive social system and forced to subsist on little food, Indians found solace and strength chewing coca leaves.

This reasoning has its appeal, but the evidence from Spanish America does not support it. Disruptions in nutritional regimes did occur, although they more frequently involved the acceptance of new foods and the loss of old ones rather than a decline in nutrition. Indians drank for many reasons, perhaps the least of which was food value, but they were fortunate that the traditional beverages were so nutritious. There is not enough evidence to prove a relationship between food shortages and drinking. If anything, drinking was more closely related to food abundance than scarcity. In the sixteenth century, new sources of animal protein and of carbohydrates reduced the dependence on traditional staples, freeing land and labor for the production of highly desirable beverages.
beverages.

Many countervailing forces determined Indian diets in the sixteenth century. New foods and more abundant supplies of nutritious beverages created the conditions for one of the best diets in the world at that time. Meat, sugar cane, and bananas along with dozens of other foods contributed proteins, carbohydrates, minerals, and vitamins. Counter-pressures in the form of new labor and tribute demands, coupled with the possible negative effects of new crops and animals, had the potential to minimize these gains. In some cases they certainly did, but through much of the central regions the evidence supports the idea of adequate if not abundant diets. Indians did not lead lives of hunger and malnutrition.

Yet the evidence in many ways remains superficial. Conquest and colonization battered Indian societies, causing changes that altered the old ways forever. The extent of these changes in the sixteenth century, at least in relation to food production and consumption, defies quantification. Much depended on the ability of Indians to maintain control over their resources, especially land and labor. It is difficult to determine how much land Indians actually lost or how many of them actually worked in the new wage system. The subsequent history of Spanish America, especially in the nineteenth century when Indians came under intense pressure, suggests that European control in the sixteenth century was limited. If most Indians did maintain control over their nutritional destiny, their diets were as good as they wanted them to be.

7

Conclusion

In pre-conquest Mesoamerica and the Andes, dense populations were supported by intensive agriculture and a sophisticated food distribution system. Agricultural achievements came in spite of the geographic obstacles of high plateaus and narrow valleys. Intensive use of the land and carefully planned distribution arrangements ensured enough food for population expansion. All came without draft animals or agricultural implements as basic as the plow. Truly remarkable civilizations had been built on the surplus agricultural production of American cereals and tubers. Tensions within these societies proved all was not well, but much had been accomplished. Not enough, though, to withstand the European conquest.

Expansion

After initial hesitation, Spaniards burst into Mesoamerica and the Andes with a speed and intensity that are still difficult to comprehend. It was a dynamic process, startling in its scope and impact. Spaniards and their plants and animals launched nutritional changes that surpassed anything that had yet been seen. Grains and livestock were only the most visible of scores of new foods that quickly became part of the emerging nutritional regimes. Each in its own way contributed to the growing supply of foods. It is unlikely that any other region in the world in the sixteenth century had such a diversity of staples and abundance of animal protein as Spanish America.

Spaniards were able to move so fast and build so much for many reasons. One essential reason was the supply of foods, the nutrients that were transformed into muscle and energy. The geographic expansion of European society was made possible because of the food supply. From Veracruz (1519), Spaniards struck for Mexico City (1521), and then north to Querétaro (1531), Durango (1531), Guadalajara (1542), and Zacatecas (1547). South and east more cities were taken or built: Puebla (1531), Oaxaca (1528), Mérida (1542), Guatemala City (1524), Chiapas (1531). Expansion in South America was equally remarkable. From Panama (1519), expeditions shot south, taking or founding Piura (1532), Cuzco (1534), Quito (1534), Lima (1535), Bogotá (1538), Santiago (1541), and Potosí (1545). By the middle of the century, Spaniards had taken much of what they wanted. By the end of the century they had pushed far beyond, establishing toeholds from the desolate northern rim of Mexico to the vast subarctic tracts of southern Chile and Argentina. Further expansion took place in the same way, drawing food supplies from the surpluses of the settled zones.

In and around the new settlements went on the many activities of colonization. Expeditions continued to probe the unknown, while forts and missions guarded the frontier. Haciendas and plantations produced foods, fibers, and dyes; *obrajes* made cloth for the local population. Scores of artisan, retail, and wholesale enterprises rebuilt much of the Old World in the New. Gold and silver mines yielded their riches, making Spanish America a prize worth defending. All this was possible so quickly because the basic food needs of Europeans and Indians were easily satisfied.

In this sense, Spanish America fulfilled what Pierre Chaunu identified as a basic motive for European expansion: the search for space to satisfy the food and energy needs left unfulfilled by an increasingly inadequate European agricultural system.[1] The agricultural surplus supported the production of goods basic to the expanding world economy. Energy had to be produced in maize and cassava fields before it could be expended in mines and plantations. Transporting food from producer to worker was always a vital part of local and regional trade. Island traders carrying cassava bread and lard in the Caribbean, mule trains transporting whitefish and snapper to Mexico City, llamas straining under loads of grain and fruits in the Andes, all were the basis of support for a much wider trading system. Precious metals, dyes, spices, and luxury foods entered the Atlantic economy as quickly as they did in the sixteenth century because of the surplus of grains, tubers, and animals in Spanish America.

The agricultural surplus did not eliminate hunger in the New World or the Old. But in Spanish America hunger was episodic, restricted to certain localities and times. Early voyages of exploration and conquest faced hunger. When it became extreme, settlers and Indians suffered.[2] Mining camps and tropical ports could suffer a "great extremitie for want of victuals" when supply routes were interrupted.[3] Weather threatened food supplies more than human behavior. Weather was overriding, uncontrollable, and unpredictable in the short term. Nevertheless, as sixteenth-century observers noted, when particularly severe weather affected one region, others often escaped and were able to help supply the nutritional needs of the affected region.[4]

Hunger seldom turned into famine and starvation. Examples of a "Jamestown fiasco," that "starving time" when immigrants succumbed to hunger, might be found, but they would not be typical.[5] In contrast to Europe, Spanish America escaped an annual period of "semi-starvation," that awful wait between the depletion of last year's food supply and the new harvest.[6] It also escaped the European famines that "constantly visited the continent laying it waste and destroying lives."[7] France with its thirteen famines in the sixteenth century was not unusual among European countries.[8] Supposedly, food problems were "far worse in Asia, China, and India."[9] Climate, disease, and lack of food conspired against Old World peoples. It was not until the eighteenth century that the European population broke through the old ceilings on growth. Appropriately enough, Europe only emerged from its cycles of hunger after incorporating the American "miracle foods" of maize and potatoes into its food regimes.[10] These and other foods helped Spanish America avoid the pain of famine so frequently felt in other parts of the world.

In contrast to Spanish America, Spain in the sixteenth century entered a prolonged period of grain shortages. At the moment of discovery Spain was already looking outward for grain, first east toward the Levant, then north toward the Baltic.[11] "Grain was a preoccupation simply because it was always scarce, a matter of life and death."[12] The situation deteriorated through the century, as Spain agonized over its predicament. To help alleviate domestic shortages, monarchs even turned to their enemies, relying on shrewd foreign policy to obtain new supplies of grain.[13]

While Spain hoped for grain from abroad, it both stymied and stimulated agriculture in its new colonies. With Columbus's second voyage went everything necessary to create agricultural self-sufficiency. Later, in order to protect favored peninsular farmers, grapes for wine and olives for oil were prohibited. The policy worked better in Mexico than in Peru, but neither region developed the distinctive Spanish reliance on wine and olive oil. The fight against wine and olives actually had little import for the self-sufficiency of the central regions. Reliance on Spain meant shortages for a very small group when trade was interrupted. Most of the population used grease and lard instead of olive oil and drank local wines and beers instead of imported ones.

Spanish America benefited from the food surpluses of the sixteenth century. Even though some outposts and ports depended on long-distance transport for foods, most of the central areas met their own subsistence needs. In addition to climatic advantages, Spanish America had more than one primary subsistence food. Maize, cassava, wheat, barley, and gradually rice were the staples anchoring diets. Even in bad times, one of these could usually be counted on for carbohydrates, with protein coming from cattle, sheep, or pigs. During normal times, grain surpluses were shipped from the highland valleys of the Andes or Mexico to the grain-dependent tropical lowlands.

Politics and Nutrition

Adequate food supplies had little to do with the apparently universal drive to monopolize food resources in the hopes of earning good profits. Charges and counter-charges of hoarding and profiteering were hurled by all. To address the problems, food politics concentrated on the distribution of food. Influential and powerful *fieles ejecutores* forced grain to market, lowered prices, and confiscated spoiled foods, acts that improved the quality of life for many. The evidence for this type of action is too extensive to dismiss it as only the response of a few individuals to specific circumstances. The creation of *alhóndigas, pósitos,* and *abastos de carne* provided the institutional framework of food security in towns large and small. The regulatory apparatus, despite its flaws, was an inexpensive way to try and resolve the daily problems of food distribution.

Problems of distribution did not necessarily lead to hunger, and food-regulating mechanisms did not arise only as a reaction to scarcity. If they had, the Mexican *albóndiga* would have been established in the late 1550s, when high prices already evoked cries of anguish from consumers. The *pósito*, the only food institution with the potential of combating famine, would have been in continuous operation. There would have been no need for the *abasto de carne*, since meat was so plentiful during most of the century.

Food regulation gave Spaniards more control over their destiny. Regulation of food, like regulation of roads, bridges, country inns, and lighting helped define the Spanish presence more clearly. Given the Spanish political tradition, it is inconceivable that food would not have been regulated. Colonization would have been incomplete without institutions and individuals entrusted with the food supply.

It is difficult to prove that the regulatory apparatus brought political rewards. But it is not too much to assume that the political and social stability of the colonies was in part attributable to the politics of provisioning. A population with adequate food is not necessarily a docile one, but when there is regular political intervention that supports rather than undermines the nutritional needs of the public the prevailing order is easier to maintain.

Food distribution laws did not have the same social overtones as laws regulating other aspects of life. According to law, everything from clothing to residence patterns to punishments differed for Spaniards and Indians. Foods laws lacked the same social implications. Only in the case of Indian drinking, and occasionally with meat, did the law try to enforce separate consumption patterns for Indians and Spaniards. In a legalistic society that was conscious of every nuance of social and ethnic status, the absence of this type of food legislation is interesting. One possible explanation is that culture defined Indian eating practices so rigidly that there was little need for Spanish law to do so. The evidence disproves this, as Indians ate and drank most Spanish foods. Another explanation is that most foods, both Indian and Spanish, were so readily available that distinctions based on who ate them were meaningless. Spaniards had a casual attitude toward food, at least compared with the Chinese, French , or even the Aztecs. They did not try to build social rank around different foods in the sixteenth century. It was not necessary, since so many other qualities determined an individual's place in society. As food supplies changed, however, distinctions did emerge. The economic reality of colonization gradually restricted Indians to the less appealing cuts of meat and coarser breads. This process was beginning at the end of the sixteenth century. By the end of the eighteenth century, a well-developed hierarchy existed.

Just how dietary differences influenced nutrition and health is not clear. Today, the poor suffer from their diets. In the sixteenth century, and even into the eighteenth, it is possible in some cases to argue that the diet of the poor was nutritionally comparable and in some cases superior to that of the wealthy. Portuguese and English planters, for example, loved imported foods and drinks as much as they did imported clothes. For dinner, they ate pickled and salted beef, pork, and fish, served with hardtack, conserves, and sweetmeats. It was the lucky barrel that arrived at Bahia or Kingston without deteriorating under the tropical sun. Europeans went ahead and ate the stinking imported foods, ignoring the cheap, readily available, and fresh local replacements. English planters in the Caribbean might have been the most profligate and extravagent of colonial diners. They consumed such quantities of food and drink that "their own intemperance" led to early sickness and death.[14] As a rule, colonial elites preferred food and drink from home when they could get it. This might have led to the paradoxial situation of the most poorly fed being the best fed. In Brazil, blacks and poor people ate local foods rich in nutrients instead of expensive imported foods.[15] Elsewhere, Indians ate fewer sweets, fats, and processed grains than Europeans, and thus may have had a superior diet.[16] Food experts in Mexico in the eighteenth century recognized the higher quality of the less refined, cheaper breads, which were usually eaten by the poor.[17] Prices defined perceptions of quality. In Mexico City in 1803, one *real* bought 21 ounces of mutton and 72 ounces of bull meat. In hospitals, when mutton was not available, larger rations of beef had to be given in order to insure that the patient received the same nutrients.[18] Fortunately for the poor, the values of the rich had little to do with the nutritional quality of food, which gave the poor the chance of receiving more nutrients per peso than the rich.

I hesitate to apply this argument to the sixteenth century. Only the broadest outline of a social hierarchy of food is visible, and its nutritional consequences are difficult to document. There were "Indian" and "Spanish" foods, but with the exception of wheat and a few luxury foods it might be more correct to emphasize an American diet rather than Indian and Spanish ones. Meat was the great equalizer here, providing nutrients for all, regardless of race and social position. Compared to grains, legumes, and fruits, meat provided much more protein and, often, more vitamins and minerals per unit consumed. It had the added advantage of being cheaper to produce than grain. The close relationship between income and protein consumption that supposedly existed in Europe did not apply to Spanish America.[19] While the European poor subsisted on protein-deficient diets, the New World poor ate much meat. They were usually able to do so without sacrificing other foods.

Abundant meat was almost as novel for Spaniards as for Indians. In addition to eating more meat, Spaniards substituted animal fats for olive oil. The use of lard, known as *grasa de vaca* and *manteca de cerdo*, was a widespread change, which struck at the very core of cultural and religious perceptions about diet. In recognition of the meat basis of the diet, Pope Pius III in 1562 granted colonists a special thirty-year exemption from fasting obligations. The end of the exemption did not bring an end to animal fats in the diet during fasting. Instead, the consumption of animal foods expanded to include eggs, cheese, milk, and butter, all usually referred to as *lacticinios*. Cultural sanctions against the use of animal products during fasting had little success, as Spaniards and Indians continued to consume meat and *lacticinios* until the end of the colonial period.[20]

The social and political system did not encourage and perpetuate limited access to foods in order to maintain control over a physically weak population. At least it would be hard to find the evidence to support such an interpretation. Social stratification often has a nutritional dimension, but the particular conditions of sixteenth-century Spanish America did not create a nutritionally weakened subordinate class. Indian or European, rich or poor, most of the population enjoyed an opportunity for nutritional well-being unmatched in recent times.

There are two qualifications to this interpretation. First, the system of poor relief seemed to institutionalize inadequate diets. Food laws precisely defined the qualities of meats and breads. Short-weighted, adulterated, waterlogged and stale bread, along with diseased, rotting meat, fed the destitute in jails and hospitals.[21] For those who were entirely dependent on food relief, nutritional inequality existed.

More difficult to analyze is Indian drinking. Conclusions depend on what is emphasized. As stated, my opinion is that Indian drinking increased with colonization. Indians did not necessarily drink more than Europeans, but they did drink more than they had before the conquest. The nutritional implications might have been positive, since *chicha* and pulque contain valuable quantities of nutrients. Rather than a compensation for food shortages, the increased use of *chicha* and pulque was a reaction to the new circumstances of the sixteenth century. Land and labor were available to produce vast quantities of the beverages, and Indians had the desire and resources to consume them.

Crisis

Food surpluses created the conditions for good diets, but they did not insulate Spanish America from fundamental changes in the sixteenth century. Much has been written of the crises of the late sixteenth century, and these are at times discussed in the context of food supply. In 1951, Woodrow Borah presented a hypothesis to explain the changes. He emphasized the epidemic of 1576 as a turning point in Mexican economic history, the beginning of an economic depression that would shadow the seventeenth century. Until the 1570s, Indian tribute provided much that was needed for the establishment and growth of Spanish communities. The epidemics of the late 1570s reduced the total amount of tribute delivered and curtailed the number of laborers available for farms and ranches. Now communities faced a "serious shortage for the first time since they were founded."[22] Various political mechanisms such as the *albóndiga* and laws regulating sales failed to ease the shortages. "After 1595 the failure of production to keep pace with a still rising white population may well have meant for the first time since the Conquest of New Spain that the white element faced a deficit in foodstuffs sufficient to place its lower groups chronically on the verge of hunger."[23] Since Indians no longer supplied the necessary nutrients, Spaniards took to the land and more directly controlled the production and distribution of foodstuffs.

Bakewell provides a good analysis of Borah's ideas. Essentially, Bakewell does not see any evidence of long-term shortages of food, nor a decline in mining production due to labor shortages. Bakewell emphasizes the dynamic role of New Spain in the Atlantic economy from the 1590s to the 1620s, a time of intense commercial exchange when New Spain was consuming large amounts of European merchandise and exporting silver in return.[24] This activity, which took place during a period of pronounced population decline, is inconsistent with economic and agricultural decline. The nutritional state of workers during this time was probably not bad. Eight years after Borah published his hypothesis on depression, Borah and Cook noted that "the frightful losses in population thus enabled the Indians to wring from their masters substantial improvements in living conditions that helped eventually to reverse the demographic trend."[25]

Bakewell suggests that by the early seventeenth century New Spain had become self-sufficient in foodstuffs, a further sign of strength.[26] I agree, but I think that this had been achieved far earlier. Vicens Vives suggests 1560 as a date of self-sufficiency for Spanish America.[27] Actually, no date can be given for all of Spanish America, since the processes of conquest and colonization spanned centuries. Regions that were to become self-sufficient—mainly the temperate basins with large populations of Spaniards and Indians—had probably done so within one generation after conquest. After that time, imports had little to do with nutrition; otherwise, interruptions in trade with Spain would have spelled disaster. Imports were important for luxury goods, wines, brandies, sweetmeats, some spices, and little more.

In Central America, the emergence of the colonial order was as jarring as in Mexico. After the disruptions of conquest, epidemics in the 1550s and the "exhaustion of the early 'looting industries' " troubled the colonies.[28] More serious for food supply and prices were the populations losses of the 1570s and 1580s. This was essentially a crisis of labor and food supply, sharp enough to promote new methods of food procurement, and eventually to send Spaniards into the countryside to assume more direct control over resources.[29]

In Andean America, colonization took a similar course. The exploitive Spanish economy sapped Indian communities of resources and people. Tribute and labor, the basis of Andean wealth, declined as the population declined, creating tensions in the economy by the 1560s. More and more was expected of Indians as they had less to give.[30]

That a crisis or series of crises spread through Spanish America in the latter part of the sixteenth century seems evident. That the crises were directly related to food supply is less certain. Prices for some foods increased as the century progressed, but hunger did not automatically follow. Wages increased as prices rose, lessening some of the negative nutritional effect. Shortages or high prices of a few foods did not reflect general conditions. An increase in the price of wheat or maize in one year did not cause hunger, because Indians and Spaniards had recourse to dozens of other foods to help them overcome deficits from sporadic grain shortages. Meat, a luxury in Europe, was an everyday food that limited the spread of hunger.

The social stability of cities more than anything else reflected the adequacy of food supplies. Compared to European cities, where famine prompted mob attacks on urban food reserves, Spanish American cities were places of tranquility and order.[31] City officials during the worst years of the 1540s and 1570s worried about prices and distribution, but not about social unrest caused by food shortages, or at least they seldom expressed that concern. Hunger was an infrequent word in their vocabulary.[32]

Indians living in rural communities came under increasing attack by the end of the sixteenth century. Although some stood strong, they ultimately faced impoverishment.[33] I suggest that the strength of Indian communities depended largely on their ability to incorporate new foods into their diet. The Indian capacity to absorb new foods was great. Livestock, fowl, barley, bananas, and many other foods quickly became parts of the Indian diet without displacing old foods. Like a great river able to accept water from many tributaries without changing course, Indian diets increased in volume and variety, though the staples remained the same. Adequate food supplies helped Indians combat the new biological and social threats of the conquest.

Sixteenth-century Spanish America may have been unique. While much of the world fought against shortages and famines, Spanish America produced surplus quantities of grains and meats. It is both sad and ironic that one of the greatest population losses in history occurred during this period of good food supplies. Yet food surpluses helped Indians withstand disease and social upheaval. The surpluses also hastened conquest and colonization, aiding Spaniards to explore and build new societies. As the new societies confronted the tensions of the late sixteenth century, they could still rely on adequate food supplies.

Notes

Abbreviations Used in Notes

ACCM   *Actas de cabildo de la ciudad de México*. 50 vols. Mexico City: Ignacio
          Bejarano, 1889–1916.
AGI   Archivo General de Indias, Seville
AGN   Archivo General de la Nación, Mexico City
CDHE   *Colección de Documentos Inéditos para la Historia de España*. 113
          vols. New York: Kraus Reprints, 1964.
CDHFS   *Colección de Documentos para la Historia de la Formación Social
          de Hispanoamérica, 1493–1810*. Ed. Richard Konetzke. 3 vols. in 5.
          Madrid: Consejo Superior de Investigaciones Científicas, 1953.
CDIRDCO   *Colección de Documentos Ineditos relativos al descubrimiento, con-
          quista y organización de las Antiguas Posesiones Españoles de
          Ultramar*. Second series. 25 vols. Madrid: Real Academia de la Histo-
          ria, 1885–1932.
CVD   *Colección de los Viages y Descubrimientos que hicieron por mar los
          Españoles desde fines del Siglo XV*. Ed. Martín Fernández de Navar-
          rete. 5 vols. Buenos Aires: Editorial Guaranía, 1945.

ENE	Paso y Troncoso, Francisco del. *Epistolario de Nueva España, 1505–1818.* 15 vols. Mexico City: José Porrua, 1939.
LCL	*Libros de cabildos de Lima, 1534–1611.* 16 vols. Lima: Torres Aguirre, 1935–48.
MNAH	Museo Nacional de Antropología e Historia, Mexico City.
PNV	Hakluyt, Richard. *The Principal Navigations, Voyages, Traffiques and Discoveries of the English Nation.* 8 vols. London and Toronto: J. M. Dent, 1927–28.
RGIP	Jiménez de la Espada, Marcos (ed.). *Relaciones geográficas de Indias: Perú.* 3 vols. Madrid: Ediciones Atlas, 1965.
RLI	*Recopilación de leyes de los reynos de las Indias.* 3 vols. Madrid: Gráficas Ultra, 1943.

Chapter One

[1]Louis Stouff, *Ravitaillement et alimentation en Provence aux 14ᵉ et 15ᵉ siècles* (Paris: Mouton, 1970); John Burnett, *Plenty and Want: A Social History of Diet in England from 1815 to the Present* (London: Thomas Nelson, 1966); Richard Osborn Cummings, *The American and His Food. A History of Food Habits in the United States* (Chicago: The University of Chicago Press, 1941). A somewhat comparable Latin American work is Berta Cabanillas de Rodriguez's *El puertorriqueño y su alimentación a través de su historia: siqlos XVI a XIX* (San Juan: Instituto de Cultura Puertorriqueña, 1973).

[2]Richard N. Adams wrote what may have been the first serious attempt to interpret the influence of food on Latin American history. "Food Habits in Latin America: A Preliminary Historical Survey," in Iago Galdston (ed.), *Human Nutrition: Historic and Scientific* (New York: International Universities Press, 1960), especially pp. 7–10; George Kubler has discussed why Indians accepted or rejected new foods in "The Quechua in the Colonial World," in Julian H. Steward (ed.), *Handbook of South American Indians* (Washington, D.C.: Smithsonian Institution, 1946), vol. 2, pp. 354–59; Sherburne F. Cook and Woodrow Borah have written the most comprehensive study of dietary change in the sixteenth century. *Essays in Population History,* vol. 3, *Mexico and California* (Berkeley and Los Angeles: University of California Press, 1979), pp. 129–176, especially pp. 142 and 160 for references to the continuity of diets.

[3]Caio Prado Júnior, *The Colonial Background of Modern Brazil,* tr. Suzette Macedo (Berkeley and Los Angeles: University of California Press, 1969), pp. 187–88.

[4]Josué de Castro, *The Geography of Hunger* (Boston: Little, Brown and Company, 1952), p. 77.

[5]Benjamin Keen, in his introduction to Alonso de Zorita, *Life and Labor in Ancient Mexico* (New Brunswick: Rutgers University Press, 1963), pp. 64–66; Carlos Malpica Silva Santisteban, *Crónica del hambre en el Perú* (Lima: Moncloa Campodónico Ediciones, 1970), pp. 70–71; Alejandra Moreno Toscano, "Tres problemas en la geografía del maíz, 1600–1624," *Historia Mexicana,* 14:4 (April–June,

1964), pp. 639–42. By the late eighteenth century, agricultural reformers worried that plantation societies usually experienced food shortages. J. H. Galloway, "Agricultural Reform and the Enlightenment in Late Colonial Brazil," *Agricultural History*, 53:4 (October., 1979), pp. 772–73.

⁶Nicolás Sánchez-Albornoz, *The Population of Latin America*, tr. W.A.R. Richardson (Berkeley and Los Angeles: University of California Press, 1974), p. 60. In early writings, Sherburne F. Cook and Woodrow Borah also pointed to a "deterioration in nutrition" as one of the factors contributing to Indian population decline. "The Rate of Population Change in Central Mexico, 1550–1570," *Hispanic American Historical Review*, 37:4 (November, 1957), p. 467. For Brazil, see Thales de Azevedo, *Povoamento da Cidade do Salvador*, 2d ed. (São Paulo: Companhia Editôra Nacional, 1955), p. 214.

⁷John Duffy, *Epidemics in Colonial America* (Baton Rouge: Louisiana State University Press, 1953), p. 11.

⁸Cook and Borah, *Essays*, vol. 3, pp. 129–176.

⁹Charles Gibson, *The Aztecs Under Spanish Rule* (Stanford: Stanford University Press, 1964), p. 308.

¹⁰Gonzalo Aquirre Beltrán, "Cultura y nutrición," in *Estudios antropolóqicos publicados en homenaje al doctor Manuel Gamio* (Mexico City: Universidad Nacional, 1956), p. 227.

¹¹Earl J. Hamilton, "Wages and Subsistence on Spanish Treasure Ships," *Journal of Political Economy*, 37 (1929), pp. 430–450; Eli F. Heckscher, *An Economic History of Sweden* (Cambridge, MA: Harvard University Press, 1954), p. 69; A. Wyczanski, "The Social Structure of Nutrition, a Case," *Acta Poloniae historica*, 18 (1968), p. 66; Eliyahu Ashtor, "An Essay on the Diet of the Various Classes in the Medieval Levant," in Robert Forster and Orest Ranum (eds.), *Biology of Man in History* (Baltimore: Johns Hopkins University Press, 1975), p. 140.

¹²Fernand Braudel, *Civilization and Capitalism. 15th–18th Century*, vol. 1, *The Structures of Everyday Life*, tr. Siân Reynolds (New York: Harper and Row, 1981), p. 130; Frederick W. Mote, "Yuan and Ming," in K. C. Chang (ed.), *Food in Chinese Culture: Anthropological and Historical Perspectives* (New Haven and London: Yale University Press, 1977), p. 198.

¹³Cook and Borah, *Essays*, vol. 3, p. 163; Woodrow Borah, "Five Centuries of Food Production and Consumption in Central Mexico," manuscript forthcoming in *Memoria de la Academia Mexicana de la Historia*, p. 21.

¹⁴Cited in Olwen Hufton, "Social Conflict and the Grain Supply in Eighteenth-Century France," *Journal of Interdisciplinary History*, 14:2 (August, 1983), p. 305.

¹⁵Harry Cross, "Living Standards in Rural Nineteenth-Century Mexico: Zacatecas 1820–80," *Journal of Latin American Studies*, 10:1 (May, 1978), pp. 1–19, *passim*.

¹⁶Luis Lisanti, "Sur la nourriture des 'Paulistes' entre XVIIIᵉ et XIXᵉ siècles," *Annales, E.S.C.*, 18:3 (May–June, 1963), pp. 535–37.

¹⁷René Salinas Meza, "Raciones alimenticias en Chile colonial," *Historia* (Santiago), 12 (1974–75), p. 75.

¹⁸John C. Super, "Spanish Diet in the Atlantic Crossing, the 1570s," *Terrae Incognitae*, 16 (1984), pp. 57–70, *passim*.

[19]René O. Craviato, "Valor nutritivo de los alimentos mexicanos," *America Indígena*, 11:4 (October, 1951), p. 298.

[20]David Noble Cook gives a very good summary of this approach in his *Demographic Collapse: Indian Peru, 1520–1620* (Cambridge: Cambridge University Press, 1981), pp. 14–29; see also William M. Denevan, "The Aboriginal Population of Amazonia," in William M. Denevan (ed.), *The Native Population of the Americas in 1492* (Madison: University of Wisconsin Press, 1976), pp. 205–34; William T. Sanders and Barbara J. Price, *Mesoamerica: The Evolution of a Civilization* (New York: Random House, 1968), p. 87.

[21]For a discussion of some of these problems see: Hugues Neveux, "L'alimentation du XIVe au XVIIIe siècle," *Revue d'Histoire Economique et Sociale*, 61 (1973), pp. 336–79; Maurice Aymard, "Pour l'histoire de l'alimentation: quelque remarques de méthode," *Annales, E.S.C.*, 30 (1975), pp. 431–444; John C. Super, "Sources and Methods for the Study of Historical Nutrition in Latin America," *Historical Methods*, 14:1 (Winter, 1981), pp. 22–30; Cook and Borah, *Essays*, vol. 3, pp. 140–167.

[22]*Cargas* of flour used for baking in eighteenth-century Mexico City weighed from 111.05 kilograms to 168.5 kilograms. AGN, Alhóndigas y Pósitos, vol. 4, 1, fols. 4–25, 21 May 1792.

[23]Susan Cotts Watkins and Etienne van de Walle analyze many of the problems in "Nutrition, Mortality, and Population Size: Malthus' Court of Last Resort," in Robert I. Rotberg and Theodore K. Rabb (eds.), *Hunger and History: The Impact of Changing Food Production and Comsumption Patterns on Society* (Cambridge: Cambridge University Press, 1985), pp. 7–28. See also A. B. Appleby, "Nutrition and Disease: The Case of London, 1550–1756," *Journal of Interdisciplinary History*, 6:1 (Summer, 1975), pp. 1–22.

[24]Woodrow Borah and Sherburne F. Cook, *Price Trends of Some Basic Commodities in Central Mexico, 1531–1570*, Ibero-Americana, 40 (Berkeley and Los Angeles: University of California Press, 1958).

[25]Enrique Florescano's study of maize prices is still one of the best historical analyses of prices available for Latin America, *Precios de maíz y crisis agrícolas en México, (1708–1810)* (Mexico City: El Colegio de México, 1969).

[26]John C. Super, "The Formation of Nutritional Regimes in Colonial Latin America," in John C. Super and Thomas C. Wright (eds.), *Food, Politics, and Society in Latin America* (Lincoln: University of Nebraska Press, 1985), pp. 1–23. See also the essay on urban provisioning by Francisco de Solano, "An Introduction to the Study of Provisioning in the Colonial City," in Richard P. Schaedel, Jorge E. Hardoy, and Nora Scott Kinzer (eds.), *Urbanization in the Americas From Its Beginnings to the Present* (The Hague: Mouton Publishers, 1978), pp. 99–129.

[27]PNV, vol. 6, p. 262.

[28]Zorita, *Life*, p. 214.

[29]ENE, vol. 4, p. 146.

[30]ENE, vol. 8, p. 104.

[31]James Lockhart and Enrique Otte, *Letters and People of the Spanish Indies: The Sixteenth Century* (Cambridge: Cambridge University Press, 1976), p. 144.

[32]Charles R. Boxer, *The Golden Age of Brazil, 1695–1750* (Berkeley and Los Angeles: University of California Press, 1964), p. 13.

[33]Frédéric Mauro, *Le XVIᵉ siècle européen: Aspects économiques* (Paris: Presses Universitaires de France, 1966), p. 177.

Chapter Two

[1]Juan López de Velasco, *Geografía y descripción universal de las Indias* (Madrid: Biblioteca de Autores Españoles, 1971), p. 9.

[2]AGI, Lima, leg. 30, 5, fol. 80v, 6 August 1582.

[3]Letter of Bernabé Cobo, 7 March 1630, in Antonio Vázquez de Espinosa, *Descripción de la Nueva España en el siglo XVII* (Mexico City: Editorial Pastria, 1944), p. 201.

[4]Miguel Alvarez Ossorio y Redín, *Con estos dos memoriales, se descubren medios para quitar los tributos y sustentar continuamente quatro millones de personas pobres* (Madrid, n.p., 1686), p. 6.

[5]Michael Nelson, *The Development of Tropical Lands: Policy Issues in Latin America* (Baltimore and London: Johns Hopkins University Press, 1973), p. 36.

[6]RGIP, vol. 2, p. 80; Pero Magalhaẽs de Gandavo, *Historia da provincia Sancta Cruz*, tr. John B. Stetson, Jr. (New York: Cortés Society, 1922), p. 48.

[7]J. H. Parry, "The Indies Richly Planted," *Terrae Incognitae*, 1 (1969), p. 20.

[8]RGIP, vol. 1, p. 132.

[9]S. Linne, "Hunting and Fishing in the Valley of Mexico in the Middle of the 16th Century," *Ethnos*, 2 (1937), pp. 58–64.

[10]José Antonio Alzate y Ramirez, *Consejos útiles para socorrer a la necesidad en tiempo que escasen los comestibles* (Mexico City: Felipe de Zuñiga y Ontiveros, 1786), p. 15.

[11]Juan de Solórzano y Pereyra, *Política Indiana* (Madrid: Compañía Ibero-Americana de Publicaciones, 1930), vol. 1, p. 45.

[12]Two very good introductions to the transatlantic food trade are Alfred W. Crosby, Jr., *The Columbian Exchange* (Westport, CT: Greenwood Press, 1972), and G. B. Masefield, "Crops and Livestock," in E. E. Rich (ed.), *Cambridge Economic History of Europe* (Cambridge: Cambridge University Press, 1967), vol. 4, pp. 276–307. Alexander von Humboldt, who "admired the extraordinary activity" of Spaniards in transferring foods to America, wrote extensively about agriculture and agricultural history. *Ensayo político sobre el reino de la Nueva España*. tr. Vito Alessio Robles (Mexico City: Editorial Pedro Robredo, 1941), vol. 3, pp. 9–93. Mariano de Carcer y Disdier lists the new foods in *Apuntes para la historia de la transculturación Indoespañola* (Mexico City: Instituto de Historia, 1953), pp. 18–19.

[13]ACCM, vol. 1, pp. 82–83.

[14]MNAH, "Testamento de Juan de la Rea, 1614–1615," Querétaro microfilm series, roll 22.

[15]Gonzalo Fernández de Oviedo, *Sumario de la natural historia de las Indias* (Mexico City: Fondo de Cultura Económica, 1950), pp. 237–39; José de Acosta,

Historia natural y moral de las Indias (Mexico City: Fondo de Cultura Económica, 1940), pp. 281–83; Humboldt, *Ensayo político*, vol. 3, pp. 18–20.

[16]José Honório Rodrigues, *Brazil and Africa*, tr. Richard A. Mazzara and Sam Hileman (Berkeley and Los Angeles: University of California Press, 1965), pp. 103–6.

[17]Pedro de Cieza de León, *La crónica del Perú* (Madrid: Espasa-Calpe, 1962), pp. 129–30; Francisco Javier Clavijero, *The History of Mexico*, tr. Charles Cullen (London: G. G. J & J. Robinson, 1787), vol. 2, p. 265.

[18]Bernabé Cobo, *Obras* (Madrid: Atlas, 1956), vol. 1, p. 426; vol. 2, pp. 315–17.

[19]Francesco Carletti, *My Voyage Around the World*, tr. Herbert Weinstock (New York: Random House, 1964), p. 44.

[20]ACCM, vol. 6, p. 215, 2 March 1556; PNV, vol. 6, pp. 262–63.

[21]Clavijero, *History*, vol. 2, p. 269.

[22]Louis Stouff, *Ravitaillement et alimentation en Provence aux 14ᵉ et 15ᵉ siècles* (Paris: Mouton, 1970), pp. 248–49; A. Pointrineau, "L'alimentation populaire en Auvergne au XVIIIᵉ siècle," *Annales, E.S.C.*, 17:2 (March–April, 1962), p. 326; Richard Osborn Cummings, *The American and His Food: A History of Food Habits in the United States* (Chicago: University of Chicago Press, 1941), pp. 17–23.

[23]Cieza de León, *Perú*, p. 272; Cobo, *Obras*, vol. 2, p. 315–18; RGIP, vol. 1, pp. 372–85, *passim*. A very good later description is in AGI, Indiferente General, leg. 1599, 1 January 1787.

[24]AGI, Patronato Real, leg. 189, 1, "Información," 3 August 1563.

[25]López de Velasco, *Geografía*, pp. 232–33.

[26]Cieza de León, *Perú*, pp. 195, 199.

[27]Juan de Torquemada, *Monarquía Indiana* (Mexico City: Editorial Salvador Chávez Hayhoe, 1943), vol. 1, p. 314; Motolonía (Toribio de Benavente), *Motolinía's History of the Indians of New Spain*, tr. Elizabeth Andros Foster (Berkeley: The Cortés Society), p. 204; Vázquez de Espinosa, *Compendium*, p. 156.

[28]Vázquez de Espinosa, *Compendium*, pp. 120–202, *passim*. Good descriptions of regional economic systems are found in Ida Altman and James Lockhart (eds.), *Provinces of Early Mexico* (Los Angeles: UCLA Latin American Center Publications, 1976).

[29]Alonso Mota y Escobar, *Descripción geográfica de los reinos de Nueva Galicia, Nueva Vizcaya y Nuevo León* (Mexico City: P. Robredo, 1940), p. 148.

[30]López de Velasco, *Geografía*, p. 196; Carletti, *Voyage*, p. 21; AGI, Lima, leg. 32, 28, 13 July 1589.

[31]RGIP, vol. 1, p. 127; vol. 2, p. 212.

[32]López de Velasco, *Geografía*, p. 172; Cieza de León, *Perú*, pp. 36–37; Carletti, *Voyage*, pp. 33–34; PNV, vol. 7, pp. 140, 142–43; Vázquez de Espinosa, *Compendium*, p. 300.

[33]AGI, Patronato Real, leg. 193, 38, 10 March 1561.

[34]CDIRDCO, vol. 22, p. 200.

[35]CDIRDCO, vol. 1, pp. 430–36.

[36]AGI, Mexico, leg. 21, 1, 1, 20 January 1587.

[37]RGIP, vol. 1, pp. 363, 377–83; Cieza de León, *Perú*, p. 272; Vázquez de Espinosa, *Compendium*, p. 632.

[38]Nicolás Sánchez-Albornoz, *The Population of Latin America*, tr. W.A.R. Richardson (Berkeley and Los Angeles: University of California Press, 1974), p. 83.

[39]For specific references to abundance see the many examples in AGI, Contaduría, leg. 498, 5.

[40]AGI, Mexico, leg. 21, 9-G, 20 April 1587; Lima, leg. 32, 22, fols. 120–21, 27 June 1589.

[41]Vázquez de Espinosa, *Compendium, passim.*

[42]Johann Boemus, *El Libro de las costumbres de todas las gentes del mundo y de las Indias*, tr. Francisco Thamara (Anvers: Martin Nucio, 1556), p. 304; Antonio de León Pinelo, *Questión moral si el chocolate quebranta el ayuno eclesiástico . . .* (Madrid: Juan González, 1636), p. 57.

[43]RGIP, vol. 2, pp. 19, 38, 170, 212, 295.

[44]Mota y Escobar, *Descripción*, p. 52; Motolinía, *Indians*, p. 270; Joannes de Laet, *L'Histoire du Nouveau Monde . . .* (Leyde: Chez Bonaventure, 1640), p. 195.

[45]Cieza de León, *Perú*, pp. 193, 211; Vázquez de Espinosa, *Compendium*, p. 519; Mota y Escobar, *Descripción*, p. 52.

[46]B. H. Slicher van Bath, *The Agrarian History of Western Europe, A.D. 500–1850*, tr. Olive Ordish (London: Edward Arnold, 1963), pp. 18, 328.

[47]Jaime Vicens Vives, *An Economic History of Spain*, tr. Frances M. López-Morillas (Princeton: Princeton University Press, 1969), p. 506.

[48]El Inca Garcilaso de la Vega, *Royal Commentaries of the Incas*, tr. Harold V. Livermore (Austin: University of Texas Press, 1966), vol. 1, p. 602.

[49]Humboldt, *Ensayo político*, vol. 3, p. 58; and *Personal Narrative of Travels to the Equinoctial Regions of America During the Years 1799–1804*, tr. Homasina Ross (London: Henry G. Bohn, 1852), vol. 1, p. 495.

[50]Jerome A. Offner, "Archival Reports of Poor Crop Yields in the Early Postconquest Texcocan Heartland and Their Implications for Studies of Aztec Period Population," *American Antiquity*, 45:4 (October, 1980), pp. 50–54.

[51]Sherburne F. Cook and Woodrow Borah, *Essays in Population History*. vol. 3, *Mexico and California* (Berkeley and Los Angeles: University of California Press, 1979), pp. 165–66; and Charles Gibson, *The Aztecs Under Spanish Rule* (Stanford: Stanford University Press, 1964), pp. 309–10.

[52]Eric Van Young, *Hacienda and Market in Eighteenth-Century Mexico: The Rural Economy of the Guadalajara Region, 1675–1820* (Berkeley and Los Angeles: University of California Press, 1981), p. 221, n. 48.

[53]David A. Brading, *Haciendas and Ranchos in the Mexico Bajío* (Cambridge: Cambridge University Press, 1978), p. 67.

[54]Cieza de León, *Perú*, p. 194.

[55]Torquemada, *Monarquía*, vol. 1, p. 10; Humboldt, *Ensayo político*, vol. 3, p. 39.

[56]Carl Ortwin Sauer, *The Early Spanish Main*, (Berkeley and Los Angeles: University of California Press, 1966), p. 242.

[57]Jean Baptiste Du Tertre, *Histoire générale, des Isles des Christophe, de la Guadeloupe, de la Martinique . . .* (Paris: Chez Jacques Langlois, 1640), p. 181.

[58]*Ibid*; and Claude D'Abbeville, *Histoire de la mission des Péres Capucins en l'Isle de Maragnan . . .* (Paris: François Huby, 1614), p. 207, 304–306.

[59]Fernández de Oviedo, *Sumario*, pp. 237–39; Humboldt, *Ensayo político*, vol. 3, pp. 23–25.

[60]Maximilien Sorre, *Les fondements biologiques de la géographie humaine; essai d'une écologie de l'homme* (Paris: A. Colin, 1971), p. 225; Crosby, *Columbian Exchange*, p. 175.

[61]Berta Cabanillas de Rodríguez, *El puertorriqueño y su alimentación a través de su historia* (San Juan: Instituto de Cultura Puertorriqueño, 1973), p. 282. For the Shipibo of Peru, an hour of labor yields 13,800 calories of bananas. Roland Bergman, "Subsistence Agriculture in Latin America," in John C. Super and Thomas C. Wright (eds.), *Food, Politics, and Society in Latin America* (Lincoln: University of Nebraska Press, 1985), p. 119.

Chapter Three

[1]Gonzalo Fernández de Oviedo, *Sumario de la natural historia de las Indias* (Mexico City: Fondo de Cultura Económica, 1950), p. 100.

[2]AGI, Patronato Real, leg. 170, 9, n.d. but probably 1496.

[3]José Gentil da Silva, *Desarrollo económico, subsistencia y decadencia en España* (Madrid: Editorial Ciencia Nueva, 1967), p. 53, n. 35; Fernand Braudel, *Civilization and Capitalism, 15th–18th Century*, vol. 1, *The Structures of Everyday Life*, tr. Siân Reynolds (New York: Harper and Row, 1981), pp. 194–97; Hugues Neveux, "L'alimentation du XIVe au XVIIIe siècle," *Revue d'Histoire Economique et Sociale*, 61 (1973), p. 358. In Languedoc, annual meat rations for rural workers dropped from 39.5 kilograms in 1480 to 18.2 kilograms in 1580–90. These very small amounts of meat had to be shared with the children. Emmanuel Le Roy Ladurie, *The Peasants of Languedoc*, tr. John Day (Urbana, IL: University of Illinois Press, 1974), pp. 102–03.

[4]Bernabé Cobo, *Obras* (Madrid: Atlas, 1956), vol. 1, p. 377.

[5]*Ibid*, vol. 1, p. 386.

[6]John E. Rouse, *The Criollo: Spanish Cattle in the Americas* (Norman: University of Oklahoma Press, 1977), p. 90.

[7]AGI, Patronato Real, leg. 170, 14, "Relación, 1512."

[8]CDIRDCO, vol. 9, p. 134.

[9]PNV, vol. 7, pp. 29–30.

[10]Antonio Vázquez de Espinosa, *Compendium and Description of the West Indies*, tr. Charles Upson Clark (Washington, D.C.: Smithsonian Institution, 1942), p. 118.

[11]AGI, Contaduría, leg. 499, 2, "Certificaciones de los descargos," 14 August 1577.

[12]ACCM, vol. 1, p. 58.

[13]François Chevalier's summary of the Mexican situation is still one of the best available: *La formation des grands domaines au Mexique* (Paris: Institut d' Ethnologie, 1952), pp. 102–45; see also José Matesanz, "Introducción de la ganadería en Nueva España, 1521–1535," *Historia Mexicana*, 14: 4 (April–June, 1965), pp. 533–36.

[14]AGI, Mexico, leg. 70, R, 8 November 1582.

[15]Lesley Byrd Simpson, *Exploitation of Land in Central Mexico in the Sixteenth Century*, Ibero Americana, 36 (Berkeley and Los Angeles: University of California, 1952), chart on frontispiece.

[16]Francesco Carletti, *My Voyage Around the World*, tr. Herbert Weinstock (New York: Random House, 1964), p. 66.

[17]LCL, vol. 13, p. 72, 3 March 1598; RGIP, vol. 1, p. 132.

[18]LCL, vol. 1, p. 134, 5 February 1537; vol. 5, p. 390, 27 January 1556.

[19]RGIP, vol. 1, p. 349; vol. 2, pp. 5, 213–14.

[20]Alonso de la Mota y Escobar, *Descripción geográfica de los reinos de Nueva Galicia, Nueva Vizcaya y Nuevo León*, (Mexico City: P. Robredo, 1940), p. 53; Bernabé Cobo, letter of 7 March 1630 in Antonio Vázquez de Espinosa, *Descripción de la Nueva España en el siglo XVII* (Mexico City: Editorial Pastria, 1944), p. 197.

[21]RGIP, vol. 2, p. 212.

[22]ACCM, vol. 6, p. 364, 4 August 1559.

[23]John C. Super, *La vida en Querétaro durante la colonia, 1531–1810* (Mexico City: Fondo de Cultura Económica, 1983), pp. 48–56.

[24]Meat deserves the emphasis in discussing sources of protein, but the availability of fish, especially in the coastal regions, should not be overlooked. Lima markets in the 1550s, for example, usually sold bream, dog-fish, horn-fish, mackerel, sardines, seabass, skate, sole, squid, and turbot. LCL, vol. 4, p. 658, 10 February 1553.

[25]AGI, Contaduría, leg. 522, "El peso de las reses . . . en Cartagena," 1578; PNV, vol. 7, pp. 29–30; vol. 6, p. 262; Félix de Azara, *Memoria sobre el estado rural del Río de la Plata y otros informes* (Buenos Aires: Editorial Bajel, 1943), pp. 7–25, *passim*.

[26]Francisco Javier Clavijero, *The History of Mexico*, tr. Charles Cullen (London: G. G. J. & J. Robinson, 1787), vol. 2, pp. 308–14.

[27]Chevalier was one of the first modern scholars to note the "extremely cheap meat" of the sixteenth century, *Formation*, pp. 114–15. Alfred W. Crosby, Jr. has also emphasized the availability of meat, stating that "by 1600 one of the cheapest foods in the American colonies was meat; the Spanish-American settlers were probably consuming more meat per capita than any other large group of non-nomadic people in the world." *The Columbian Exchange* (Westport, CT: Greenwood Press, 1972), p. 108. I would qualify the statement in two ways. First, by 1600 meat was becoming more expensive in the central areas; second, Indians and blacks were also eating enormous amounts of meat. For specific references to the examples cited see AGI, Mexico, leg. 21, 1, 9–G, 20 April 1587; ACCM, vol. 5, pp. 278–79, 12 December 1549; LCL, vol. 9, pp. 254–56, 27 June 1580; James Lockhart and Enrique Otte (eds.), *Letters and People of the Spanish Indies: The Sixteenth Century* (Cambridge: Cambridge University Press, 1976), p. 68.

[28]ACCM, vol. 1, p. 6, 15 March 1524; vol. 1, p. 81, 25 March 1526.

[29]PNV, vol. 6, p. 249; Carletti, *Voyage*, p. 66.

[30]AGN, Cédulas Reales, Originales, vol. 99, fols. 166–268, *passim*, in a report written in the 1760s summarizing some early dietary habits.

[31]PNV, vol. 6, p. 262.

[32]Price trends are based on some forty-seven contract prices recorded in ACCM. For examples, see vol. 1, p. 81, 25 March 1526; vol. 4, p. 274, 21 March 1542; vol. 9, p. 255, 2 February 1588; vol. 12, p. 353, 2 February 1597. Some of the prices are also discussed in Chevalier, *Formation*, pp. 114–15.

[33]Stuart B. Schwartz, "Colonial Brazil, c. 1580–c. 1750: Plantations and Peripheries," in Leslie Bethell (ed.), *The Cambridge History of Latin America*, vol. 2, *Colonial Latin America* (Cambridge: Cambridge University Press, 1984), vol. 2, p. 460.

[34]ACCM, vol. 12, p. 293, 30 July 1592.

[35]ACCM, vol. 12, p. 123, 23 February 1595.

[36]ACCM, vol. 12, p. 344, 16 January 1592.

[37]AGI, Mexico, leg. 21, 2-19-H, 17 July 1577; ACCM, vol. 6, p. 387, 14 February 1560.

[38]AGI, Mexico, leg. 22, 4-155, n.d., probably 1596.

[39]Silvestre Díaz de la Vega, "Discurso sobre la decadencia de la agricultura en el reyno de Nueva España," 24 July 1788, Biblioteca Nacional (Mexico), Gabinete de Manuscritos, fol. 13v.

[40]AGN, Hospitales, vol. 11, fol. 273, 15 April 1803; vol. 9, 5, fol. 87, 19 December 1809. Humboldt's calculations are interesting in this context. He determined that in the late eighteenth century, residents of Mexico City ate 92.5 kilograms of meat a year, while residents of Paris settled for about 80 kilograms. The exact figures are less important than the comparisons. Even though supplies had shrunk, they were still more plentiful than in Europe. By this time, however, Indians probably ate far less meat than in the sixteenth century. Alejandro de Humboldt, *Ensayo político sobre el reino de la Nueva España*, tr. Vito Alessio Robles (Mexico City: Editorial Pedro Robredo, 1941), vol. 2, p. 224.

[41]For observations on the availability of meat see LCL, vol. 4, p. 406, 13 July 1551; vol. 5, p. 282, 7 May 1555; vol. 5, p. 390, 27 January 1556; vol. 5, pp. 649–650, 13 August 1557; AGI, Lima, leg. 30, 5, fol. 136, 17 February 1583.

[42]Murdo J. MacLeod, *Spanish Central America: A Socioeconomic History, 1520–1720* (Berkeley and Los Angeles: University of California Press, 1973), p. 434, n.17; Constantino Bayles, "Nuevo capítulo de abastos en la América Español," *Razón y Fe: Revista Mensual Hispanoamericana*, 50: 632–33 (1950), p. 275.

[43]José de Acosta, *Historia natural y moral de las Indias* (Mexico City: Fondo de Cultura Económica, 1940), p. 318; anon., *Descripción del virreinato del Perú, crónica inédita de comienzos de siglo XVII* (Rosario: Universidad Nacional del Litoral, 1958), p. 103; Cobo, *Obras*, vol. 1, p. 384; vol. 2, p. 316.

[44]Francisco Millau, *Descripción de la provincia del Río de la Plata (1772)*, (Buenos Aires: Editora Espasa-Calpe, 1947), pp. 54–55; Alonzo Carrío de la Vandera, *El Lazarillo de Ciegos Caminantes* (Barcelona: Editorial Labor, 1973), p. 256; quote in Martin Dobrizhoffer, *An Account of the Abipones, an Equestrian People of Paraguay*, tr. Sarah Henry Coleridge (London: John Murray, 1822), vol. 1, p. 219, 220.

[45]Sixteenth-century accounts seldom comment on the comparative economics of livestock and crop agriculture. By the late eighteenth century, careful assessments were being made. Félix de Azara, in his *Memoria*, p. 8, concluded that 11

men could produce wheat worth 1534.5 pesos, compared to 5250 pesos' worth of cattle products. The wheat fed about 216 people, while just the offspring of the cattle fed 493 people.

[46]Pedro de Cieza de León, *La crónica del Perú* (Madrid: Espasa-Calpe, 1962), p. 235; Chevalier, *Formation*, pp. 56–57; Vázquez de Espinosa, *Compendium* pp. 40, 530.

[47]*Libro de las bulas y pragmáticas de los Reyes Católicos* (Madrid: Instituto de España, 1973), vol. 2, pp. 314–16.

[48]Miguel Alvarez Ossorio y Redín, *Čon estos dos memoriales, se descubren medios para quitar los tributos y sustentar continuamente quatro millones de personas pobres* (Madrid, n.p., 1686), p. 6. He recommends how to increase production in his *Discurso universal de las causas que ofenden esta monarquía* (Madrid: n.p., 1686), pp. 6–13.

[49]Jaime Vicens Vives, *Historia social y económica de España y América* (Barcelona: Editorial Teide, 1957), vol. 4, p. 163.

[50]Fernand Braudel, *Civilization and Capitalism*, vol. 1, *The Structures of Everyday Life*, tr. Siân Reynolds (New York: Harper and Row, 1981), p. 137.

[51]Francisco Hernández, *Historia de las plantas de Nueva España* (Mexico City: Imprenta Universitaria, 1959), vol. 2, pp. 872–73.

[52]Joannes de Laet, *L'Histoire du Nouveau Monde* (Leyde: Chez Bonaventure, 1640), pp. 239–41.

[53]John Gerard, *The Herball, or Generall Historie of Plantes* (London: Norton, 1597), p. 77.

[54]Fernández de Oviedo, *Sumario*, p. 94.

[55]Antonio de León Pinelo, *Questión moral si el chocolate quebranta el ayuno eclesiástico* (Madrid: Viuda de Juan González, 1636), p. 57.

[56]AGI, Contaduría, leg. 1519, provides examples of reactions to maize.

[57]*Diario de México* (Mexico City: Imprenta de Doña María Fernández Jáuregui, 1805–1811), vol. 4, pp. 235–36, 28 October 1806.

[58]CDIRDCO, vol. 4, p. 80; vol. 10, p. 309.

[59]ACCM, vol. 2, p. 61, 1 August 1530. Enrique Florescano has written a good survey of the expansion of wheat in sixteenth-century Mexico. He emphasizes low productivity during the early years because of the reluctance of Indians to plant. The quick drop in prices a few years after the conquest, however, suggests that the supply was sufficient for local needs. "El abasto y la legislación de granos en el siglo XVI," *Historia Mexicana*, 14:4 (April–June, 1965), pp. 571–72.

[60]Charles Gibson, *The Aztecs Under Spanish Rule* (Stanford: Stanford University Press, 1964), p. 323.

[61]Motolinía (Toribio de Benavente), *Motolinía's History of the Indians of New Spain*, tr. Elizabeth Andros Foster (Berkeley: The Cortés Society), p. 270; Juan de Torquemada, *Monarquía Indiana* (Mexico City: Editorial Salvador Chávez Hayhoe), vol. 1, pp. 9, 318; Vázquez de Espinosa, *Compendium*, pp. 134–37; Ross Hassig, *Trade, Tribute, and Transportation: The Sixteenth-Century Political Economy of the Valley of Mexico* (Norman: University of Oklahoma Press, 1985), p. 224.

[62]AGI, Mexico, leg. 2770, Juan de Castaniza, 8 January 1771; "Consejo de Indias," 2 March 1773.

[63]Mota y Escobar, *Descripción*, p. 52; Super, *Querétaro*, pp. 54–55; Vázquez de Espinosa, *Compendium*, pp. 184–91; *passim.*

[64]RGIP, vol. 1, pp. 123–247, *passim*; Vázquez de Espinosa, *Compendium*, pp. 353–553, *passim.*

[65]In the port of Paita, for example, the six or eight Spanish residents were supposedly "all traders in hardtack." RGIP, v. 1, p. 125.

[66]*Descripción del Perú*, p. 48.

[67]Cobo, *Obras*, vol. 2, p. 315.

[68]ACCM, vol. 11, p. 39, 16 November 1592.

[69]AGN, Historia, vol. 135, fol. 82, 17 April 1793; Alhóndigas y Pósitos, vol. 4, 1, fols. 139–144, 26 March 1793.

[70]Anne-Marie Puiz, "Alimentation populaire et sous-alimentation au XVIIe siècle. Le cas de Genève et de sa région," in Jean-Jacques Hémardinquer (ed.), *Pour une histoire de l'alimentation* (Paris: Cahiers de Annales, 1970), p. 140; J. C. Drummond and Anne Wilbraham, *The Englishman's Food: A History of Five Centuries of English Diet* (London: Alden Press, 1939), pp. 51, 83–84, 128; R. A. McCance and E. M. Widdowson, *Breads White and Brown: Their Place in Thought and Social History* (London: Pitman Medical Publishing Co., 1956), pp. 9–19.

[71]RGIP, vol. 1, p. 380.

[72]LCL, vol. 5, p. 48, 23 June 1553; Miguel Alvarez Ossorio y Redín, *Con estos dos memoriales, se descubren medios para quitar los tributos y sustentar continuamente quatro millones de personas pobres* (Madrid, n. p., 1686), p. 6.

[73]ACCM, vol. 1, pp. 146–47, 27 September 1527; Chevalier, *Formation*, pp. 72–77.

[74]AGI, Mexico leg. 19, 1, 21B, 30 January 1559.

[75]These trends are based on twenty-seven prices recorded in ACCM. As examples, see vol. 2, p. 61, 1 August 1530; vol. 2, p. 163, 9 February 1532; vol. 11, p. 124, 14 June 1593.

[76]ACCM, vol. 4, p. 137, 9 July 1538; vol. 4, p. 288, 16 June 1542; vol. 3, p. 54, 22 September 1533; vol. 5, p. 55, 10 July 1544; vol. 5, p. 181, 23 May 1547; vol. 5, pp. 44–45, 15 May 1544.

[77]ACCM, vol. 7, p. 181, 9 March 1564; vol. 8, p. 65, 15 June 1573; vol. 11, 11 May 1593, p. 110; 12 May 1593, pp. 111–12.

[78]AGI, Mexico, leg. 23, 1–4, 30 June 1595.

[79]LCL, vol. 4, pp. 156–57, 30 July 1549; vol. 4, pp. 403–04, 10 July 1551.

[80]LCL, vol. 9, pp. 21–22, 23 January 1579.

[81]LCL, vol. 10, p. 358, 14 July 1586; vol. 10, p. 411, 10 January 1587.

[82]In 1590 one contract called for the shipment of twenty-nine cartloads of Bajío wheat to Mexico City. MNAH, Juan Pérez de Aguilar, 28 July 1590, Querétaro microfilm series, roll 3. For Peru, see LCL, vol. 9, p. 635, 1 February 1583.

[83]*Descripción del Perú*, p. 25; Chevalier, *Formation*, p. 77.

[84]See for example the transformations in European agriculture in the early sixteenth century. B. H. Slicher van Bath, *The Agrarian History of Western Europe*, tr. Olive Ordish (London: Edward Arnold, 1963), pp. 199, 202–05.

[85]Cobo, *Obras*, vol. 2, p. 315.

[86]ACCM, vol. 1, pp. 82–83, 13 April 1526; vol. 5, p. 97, 3 July 1545; vol. 6, p. 215, 2 March 1556.

Chapter Four

[1]Francisco Domínguez y Compañy, "Funciones económicas del cabildo colonial hispano-americano," in Rafael Altamira y Crevea, *et al.*, *Contribuciones a la historia municipal de América* (Mexico City: Instituto Panamericano de Geografía e Historia, 1951), p. 144.

[2]Quoted in Mario Gongora, *Studies in the Colonial History of Spanish America* (Cambridge: Cambridge University Press, 1975), p. 71.

[3]Diego de Encinas, *Cedulario Indiano* (Madrid: Ediciones Cultura Hispánica, 1945), vol. 4, pp. 236–40.

[4]Steven L. Kaplan, *Bread, Politics, and Political Economy in the Reign of Louis XV* (The Hague: Martinus Nijhoff, 1976), vol. 1, p. xvi.

[5]Christopher Columbus, *Journals and Other Documents of the Life and Voyages of Christopher Columbus*, ed. Samuel Eliot Morison (New York: The Heritage Press, 1963), p. 88.

[6]CVD, vol. 2, pp. 196–99; Columbus, *Journals*, pp. 34–36; CDIRDCO, vol. 9, p. 377; vol. 10, pp. 19–20.

[7]CVD, vol. 2, p. 241; *Libro de las bulas y pragmáticas de los Reyes Católicos* (Madrid: Instituto de España, 1973), vol. 2, pp. 314–16.

[8]AGN, Alhóndigas y Pósitos, vol. 4, 1, fol. 90, 18 August 1792.

[9]CVD, vol. 2, pp. 241, 251–52; vol. 3, p. 508.

[10]CDIRDCO, vol. 9, p. 377; vol. 10, pp. 19–20, 244.

[11]CVD, vol. 2, pp. 216, 240.

[12]CDIRDCO, vol. 22, pp. 204–5; Hernán Cortés, *Cartas de relación de la conquista de Méjico* (Madrid: Espasa-Calpe, 1942), vol. 2, pp. 109, 126.

[13]Jaime Vicens Vives, *An Economic History of Spain*, tr. Frances M. López-Morillas (Princeton: Princeton University Press, 1969), pp. 302–5.

[14]CDIRDCO, vol. 4, p. 80; vol. 10, p. 309; CDHE, vol. 2, p. 208.

[15]AGI, Patronato Real, leg. 170, 61, various registers, 1573.

[16]Juan de Solórzano y Pereyra, *Política Indiana* (Madrid: Compañía Ibero-Americana de Publicaciones, 1930), vol. 1, p. 205.

[17]CDHFS, vol. 1, pp. 40, 47; Bartolomé de las Casas, *Historia de las Indias* (Mexico City: Fondo de Cultura Económica, 1951), vol. 2, p. 483; Luís dos Santos Vilhena, *A Bahia no século XVIII* (Bahia: Editôra Itapua, 1969), pp. 158–59.

[18]Roberto Levillier (ed.), *Gobernantes del Perú: Cartas y papeles, siglo XVI* (Madrid: Sucesores de Rivadeneyra, 1921–1926), vol. 3, p. 430, 10 June 1570.

[19]CDIRDCO, vol. 22, pp. 127–30; AGI, Lima, leg. 108, "Instrucción," 22 December 1574.

[20]ACCM vol. 12, pp. 108–10, 10 January 1595.

[21]ACCM, vol. 1, p. 13, 3 June 1524; vol. 1, pp. 22–23, 8 November 1524; AGI, Mexico, leg. 2779, "Ordenanzas de Fiel Ejecutoría, 1728" quote in José María Ots y

Capdequí, *Instituciones* (Barcelona: Salvat Editores, 1959), p. 277; Solórzano y Pereyra, *Política*, vol. 4, p. 13. Domínguez y Compañy, "Funciones," pp. 149–50.

[22]AGI, Mexico, leg. 70, 2, n.d., Estevan de Porras, probably 1582; ACCM, vol. 13, pp. 105–6, 16 January 1598. Eventually, the many *ordenanzas* passed for good government would include sections on food traders. LCL, vol. 12, "Ordenanzas hechas por el Virrey Don Garcia Hurtado de Mendoza," pp. 666–68, 24 January 1594.

[23]*Actas capitulares del ayuntamiento de la Habana*, Emilio Roig de Leuchsenring (ed.) (Havana: Municipio de la Havana, 1937), vol. 2, p. 60.

[24]ACCM, vol. 3, p. 18, 10 March 1533; vol. 6, p. 60, 18 July 1552; LCL, vol. 4, p. 69, 8 February 1549; vol. 4, pp. 424–25, 17 August 1551.

[25]AGI, Mexico, leg. 20, 1, 8, 25 December 1578; leg. 24, 1–8, 25 April 1598.

[26]LCL, vol. 6, p. 238, 11 December 1559; ACCM, vol. 1, pp. 82–83, 20 April 1526; RLI, Lib. 4, Tit. 9, Ley, 22 (vol. 2, pp. 32–33).

[27]ACCM, vol. 1, p. 48, 26 July 1525; RGIP, vol. 2, p. 300; Solórzano y Pereyra, *Política*, vol. 1, pp. 240–50; RLI, Lib. 4, Tit. 17, Ley 1 (vol. 2, p. 56).

[28]AGN, Alhóndigas y Pósitos, vol. 14, 1, fols. 1–21, beginning 15 February 1673.

[29]LCL, vol. 4, p. 336, 12 January 1551; vol. 12, "Ordenanzas hechas por el Virrey Don García Hurtado de Mendoza," pp. 677–79, 24 January 1594.

[30]AGI, Mexico, leg. 2779, "Ordenanzas de Fiel Ejecutoría, 1728."

[31]CDIRDCO, vol. 22, p. 142; ACCM, vol. 2, p. 193, 6 September, 1532; vol. 3, pp. 58–59, 31 October 1533; vol. 6, pp. 196–99, 26 November 1555; vol. 7, p. 470, 9 February 1570.

[32]LCL, vol. 5, p. 236, 2 January 1555.

[33]ENE, vol. 8, p. 102; ACCM, vol. 7, p. 45, 29 April 1562.

[34]AGI, Mexico, 2779, "Ordenanzas de Fiel Ejecutoría, 1728"; CDIRDCO, vol. 6, p. 339.

[35]CDIRDCO, vol. 5, pp. 23–28; vol. 9, p. 21; Encinas, *Cedulario*, vol.1, pp. 179–201.

[36]Encinas, *Cedulario*, vol. 3, pp. 428–445.

[37]AGI, Quito, leg. 8, 15 April 1595; RLI, Lib. 8, Tit. 13 (vol. 2, pp. 498–510); Encinas, *Cedulario*, vol. 3, pp. 428–445.

[38]Encinas, *Cedulario*, vol. 3, p. 449; ACCM, vol. 7, 25 September 1566.

[39]AGI, Lima, leg. 108, 21 May 1592.

[40]ACCM, vol. 4, p. 207, 3 September 1540; vol. 4, p. 333, 15 March 1543; vol. 8, p. 84, 20 November 1573.

[41]LCL, vol. 6, pt. 2, p. 491, 8 April 1567; Marqués de Montemira, "Representación . . . que la sisa" (Lima: Imprenta Real de los Niños Expósitos, 1789), p. 18.

[42]Eighteenth-century legislation seemed to threaten small food retailers more than sixteenth-century legislation. AGN, Alhóndigas y Pósitos, vol. 2, 126, 22 October 1756; AGI Indiferente General, leg. 1693, "Copia de la Real Ordenanza," 27 February 1785.

[43]LCL, vol. 9, p. 227, 25 April 1580; ACCM, vol. 13, p. 94, 29 December 1597; vol. 14, p. 154, 27 October 1600.

[44]LCL, vol. 5, p. 283, 10 May 1555.

[45]ACCM, vol. 7, pp. 364–365, 12 September 1567; vol. 8, p. 500, 12 June 1581; vol. 8, pp. 725–729, 3 December 1584. Enrique Florescano has written the best

discussion of the early years of grain institutions. "El abasto y la legislación de granos en el siglo XVI," *Historia Mexicana*, 14:4 (April–June, 1965), pp. 603–24. See also Irene Vásquez de Warman, "El pósito y alhóndiga en la Nueva España," *Historia Mexicana*, 17:3 (January–February, 1968), pp. 395–426. For later years, see Florescano's *Precios del maíz y crisis agrícolas en México (1708–1810)* (Mexico City: El Colegio de México, 1969), *passim*, and Eric Van Young, *Hacienda and Market in Eighteenth-Century Mexico: The Rural Economy of the Guadalajara Region, 1675–1820* (Berkeley and Los Angeles: University of California Press, 1981), pp. 59–103, *passim*.

[46]AGI, Mexico, leg. 70, 2, 10 January 1582, 7 November 1782.

[47]AGI, Alhóndigas y Pósitos, vol. 2, fols. 2–127, 22 October 1756.

[48]AGI, Lima, leg. 28 A, 63-H, fol. 3, 15 April 1574.

[49]LCL, vol. 6, p. 445, 1 August 1561.

[50]LCL, vol. 11, p. 396, 22 July 1590; vol. 12, p. 210, 11 November 1594; vol. 12, p. 216, 25 November 1594.

[51]For examples of the discussion in the context of late eighteenth-century Mexico, see AGN, Alhóndigas y Pósitos, vol. 2, fols. 160–87, 3 October 1795; *Gazetas de México*, vol. 2, pp. 185–91, 22 August 1786.

[52]ACCM, vol. 11, p. 110, 11 May, 1593; vol. 11, pp. 111–12, 12 May 1593.

[53]ACCM, vol. 11, p. 102, 26 April 1593.

[54]ACCM, vol. 12, p. 303, 26 August 1596; vol. 12, p. 373, 17 March 1597.

[55]AGI, Mexico, leg. 2770, "Juan de Castaniza," 8 January 1771; "Consejo de Indias," 2 March 1773.

[56]LCL, vol. 5, p. 282, 6 May 1555; vol. 10, p. 311, 13 March 1586; vol. 13, p. 254, 5 April 1599; ACCM, vol. 3, p. 53, 2 September 1533; vol. 8, p. 385, 4 May 1578; vol. 12, p. 293, 30 July 1596. For good regional analyses of the *abasto* in later periods see Ward Barrett, "The Meat Supply of Colonial Cuernavaca," *Annals of the Association of American Geographers*, 64:4 (December, 1974), pp. 525–45, and Van Young, *Hacienda*, pp. 49–58.

[57]ACCM, vol. 8, pp. 156–159, 27 January 1575; vol. 8, p. 250, 5 August 1578; vol. 12, p. 370, 13 March 1597.

[58]AGI, Mexico, leg. 21, 2, 19-H, 17 July 1577; leg. 23, 4–86, 4 August 1597; leg. 70, 3, 29 October 1583.

Chapter Five

[1]AGI, Mexico, leg. 70, 3, 15 April 1583.

[2]William M. Denevan (ed.), *The Native Population of the Americas in 1492* (Madison: University of Wisconsin Press, 1976), pp. 37, 152; Nicolás Sánchez Albornoz, *The Population of Latin America*, tr. W.A.R. Richardson (Berkeley and Los Angeles: University of California Press, 1974), pp. 33–35.

[3]Sherburne F. Cook and Woodrow Borah, *Essays in Population History*, vol. 3., *Mexico and California* (Berkeley and Los Angeles: University of California Press, 1979), p. 100.

[4]David Noble Cook, *Demographic Collapse: Indian Peru, 1520–1620* (Cambridge: Cambridge University Press, 1981), p. 114.

[5]AGI, Lima, leg. 2, 28, 16 June 1561; leg. 33, 36, fols. 143–44, 2 May 1599; Mexico, leg. 19, 1, 13, 7 February 1554.

[6]Elsa Malvido, "Efectos de las epidemias y hambrunas en la población colonial de México (1519–1810)," in Enrique Florescano and Elsa Malvido (comps.), *Ensayos sobre la historia de las epidemias en México* (Mexico City: Instituto Mexicano del Seguro Social, 1982), vol. 1, p. 179. For examples of the use of the term *famine* see: Miguel E. Bustamante, "Aspectos históricos y epidemiológicos del hambre en México," in the same volume, p. 37; Cook, *Demographic*, p. 172; Robert C. West and John P. Augelli, *Middle America: Its Lands and Peoples* (Englewood Cliffs, N.J.: Prentice-Hall, 1966), p. 75; Nancy M. Farriss, *Maya Society Under Colonial Rule: The Collective Enterprise of Survival* (Princeton: Princeton University Press, 1984), p. 61.

[7]Ross Hassig has written the most convincing analysis of an early Mexican famine: "The Famine of One Rabbit: Ecological Causes and Social Consequences of a Precolumbian Calamity," *Journal of Anthropological Research*, 37:2 (Spring, 1981), pp. 172–182. See also Francisco Javier Clavijero, *The History of Mexico*, tr. Charles Cullen (London: G.G. J. and J. Robinson, 1787), v. 1, p. 181; Rosaura Hernández Rodrígues, "Epidemias y calamidades en el México prehispánico," in Florescano and Malvido, *Ensayos*, vol. 1, p. 146; Carlos Viesca T., "Hambruna y epidemia en Anáhuac (1450–1454) en la época de Moctezuma Ilhuicamina," in the same volume, p. 159; Michael M. Swann, "The Demographic Impact of Disease and Famine in Late Colonial Northern Mexico," *Geoscience and Man*, 21 (1980), pp. 97–109, *passim*.

[8]Bernardino de Sahagún, *Historia general de las cosas de Nueva España* (Mexico City: Editorial Pedro Robredo, 1938), vol. 3, p. 304.

[9]M. K. Bennett, "Famine," *International Encyclopedia of the Social Sciences* (New York: The Macmillan Company and the Free Press, 1968), vol. 5, p. 322.

[10]Alfred W. Crosby, Jr. has already recognized this for the European population in his *The Columbian Exchange* (Westport, CN: The Greenwood Press, 1972), p. 108. Juan de Torquemada was one contemporary writer who was quite specific about the absence of famines. *Monarquía Indiana* (Mexico City: Editorial Salvador Chávez Hayhoe, 1943), vol. 2, p. 481.

[11]Cook and Borah, *Essays*, vol. 3, pp. 168, 172–74.

[12]Fernand Braudel, *Capitalism and Material Life*, tr. Miriam Kochan (New York: Harper and Row, 1973), p. 129.

[13]AGI, Lima, leg. 32, 56, 3 May 1592.

[14]AGI, Mexico, leg. 20, 1, 29, 18 October 1579; leg. 21, 3, 52, 4 December 1588.

[15]AGI, Mexico, leg. 22, 1–16, 5 June 1590.

[16]Oscar Lewis, *Life in a Mexican Village: Tepoztlán Restudied* (Urbana: University of Illinois Press, 1963), p. 132.

[17]Ross Hassig, *Trade, Tribute, and Transportation: The Sixteenth-Century Political Economy of the Valley of Mexico* (Norman: University of Oklahoma Press, 1985), p. 182.

[18]Carl Ortwin Sauer, *The Early Spanish Main* (Berkeley and Los Angeles: University of California Press, 1966), pp. 157, 203.

[19]François Chevalier, *La formation des grands domaines au Mexique* (Paris: Institut d'Ethnologie, 1952), pp. 244–70, *passim*. In some regions of coastal Peru,

Indians may have built mud walls to protect their crops. Robert G. Keith, *Conquest and Agrarian Change: The Emergence of the Hacienda System on the Peruvian Coast* (Cambridge: Harvard University Press, 1976), p. 64.

[20]Nicolás Sánchez-Albornoz said that livestock was "as much a pest as the plague." *Population*, p. 57; Murdo J. MacLeod, *Spanish Central America: A Socioeconomic History, 1520–1570* (Berkeley and Los Angeles: University of California Press, 1973), pp. 127–28; West and Augelli, *Middle America*, p. 287.

[21]Santiago Antúnez de Mayolo R., "La nutrición en el antiguo Perú," III Congreso Peruano, *El hombre y la cultura andina*, (Lima: Ramiro Matos M., 1977), vol. 5, p. 814.

[22]In Tlaxcala, "whole pueblos were destroyed by cattle." Charles Gibson, *Tlaxcala in the Sixteenth Century*, Stanford ed. (Stanford: Stanford University Press, 1967), p. 152. See also José Matesanz, "Introducción de la ganadería en Nueva España, 1521–1535," *Historia Mexicana*, 14:4 (April–June, 1965), p. 539; Jesús Ruvalcaba Mercado, "Agricultura colonial temprana y transformación social en Tepeapulco y Tulancingo (1521–1610), *Historia Mexicana*, 33:4 (April–June, 1984), p. 438.

[23]Marvin Harris, *Cows, Pigs, Wars and Witches. The Riddles of Culture* (New York: Vintage Books, 1978), pp. 26–27.

[24]Richard L. Garner, "Price Trends in Eighteenth-Century Mexico," *Hispanic American Historial Review*, 65:2 (May, 1985), pp. 285–87.

[25]Enrique Florescano, "The Formation and Economic Structure of the Hacienda in New Spain," in Leslie Bethell (ed.), *The Cambridge History of Latin America*. vol. 2, *Colonial Latin America* (Cambridge: Cambridge University Press, 1984), p. 155.

[26]Charles Gibson, *The Aztecs Under Spanish Rule* (Stanford: Stanford University Press, 1964), p. 567, n. 87; RGIP, vol. 2, p. 251; ACCM, vol. 6, p. 494, 3 October 1561.

[27]AGI, Lima, leg. 28A, 63–0, fols. 3v–4, 2 April 1573.

[28]Chevalier, *Formation*, pp. 58–59; Enrique Florescano, "El abasto y la legislación de granos en el siglo XVI," *Historia Mexicana*, 14:4 (April–June, 1965), p. 583; Hassig, *Trade*, p. 22.

[29]Pedro de Cieza de León, *La crónica del Perú* (Madrid: Espasa-Calpe, 1962), p. 131 is an early (1540s) reference to Indian wheat consumption. *Cabildo* records from the 1550s refer to cheap wheat bread, noting that poor people and Indians ate it. LCL, vol. 6, p. 56, 26 April 1558. Cook and Borah, *Essays*, vol. 3, p. 169. Eighteenth-century sources have many references. See for example, AGN, Historia, vol. 135, 7, fols. 81–82, 7 April 1793; Alhóndigas y Pósitos, vol. 4, 2, fols. 130–34 28 April 1795.

[30]Alejandra Moreno Toscano, "Tres problemas en la geografía del maíz, 1600–1624," *Historia Mexicana*, 14:4 (April–June, 1964), pp. 639–42.

[31]Alejandro de Humboldt, *Ensayo político sobre el reino de la Nueva España*, tr. Vito Alessio Robles (Mexico City: Editorial Pedro Robredo, 1941), vol. 2, p. 102.

[32]Ramiro Guerra y Sánchez, *Sugar and Society in the Caribbean: An Economic History of Cuban Agriculture* (New Haven: Yale University Press, 1964), pp. 38–70, *passim*.

[33]*Ibid.*, pp. 10–23, *passim*.

[34]Diego de Encinas, *Cedulario Indiano* (Madrid: Ediciones Cultura Hispánica, 1945), vol. 4, pp. 311. A good summary of the services expected from Indians is in AGI, Lima, 28B 1 March 1572, especially 27–30v.

[35]The term is Karen Spaldings, *Huarochiri: An Andean Society Under Inca and Spanish Rule* (Palo Alto: Stanford University Press, 1984), pp. 134–35. For good discussions of the issues involved see MacLeod, *Central America*, pp. 206–226, and Linda A. Newson, "Demographic Catastrophe in Sixteenth-Century Honduras," in David J. Robinson (ed.), *Studies in Spanish American Population History* (Boulder, CO: Westview Press, 1981), pp. 231–34.

[36]Motolinía (Toribio de Benavente), *Motolinía's History of the Indians of New Spain*, tr. Elizabeth Andros Foster (Berkeley: The Cortés Society, 1950), pp. 42–43; AGI, Mexico, leg. 3, 122, 10 May 1586.

[37]Jeffrey A. Cole, *The Potosí Mita, 1573–1700* (Palo Alto: Stanford University Press, 1985), pp. 3–6, 30–32; AGI, Lima, leg. 31, 17, fols. 18, 42v–43.

[38]AGI, Lima, leg. 19, 17, fols. 1–48, report begins 12 July 1595.

[39]AGI, Lima, leg. 32, 36, fols. 39–40, ? April 1590; RGIP, vol. 2, p. 292; ENE, vol. 3, p. 187; "Aranzel de los jornales que se han de pagar a los indios," (Lima, n.p., 1687); RLI, Lib. 6, Tit. 1, Ley 26; and Lib. 6, Tit. 12, Ley 28 (vol. 2, pp. 195, 292).

[40]AGI, Mexico, leg. 24, 1–6C, "Utilidades e inconbenientes," n.d., probably 1598.

[41]AGI, Lima, leg. 28A, 1, 10 June 1570; Lima, leg. 33, 36, 16, fols. 84–86v, January 1599.

[42]Chevalier, *Formation*, p. 133.

[43]RGIP, vol. 2, p. 311.

[44]Peter Bakewell, "Mining in Colonial Spanish America," in Leslie Bethell (ed.), *The Cambridge History of Latin America*, vol. 2, *Colonial Latin America* (Cambridge: Cambridge University Press, 1984), pp. 127–28; and his *Miners of the Red Mountain: Indian Labor in Potosí, 1545–1650* (Albuquerque: University of New Mexico Press, 1984), pp. 182–83.

[45]Steve Stern, *Peru's Indian Peoples and the Challenge of Spanish Conquest* (Madison: The University of Wisconsin Press, 1982), p. 87; Bakewell, *Miners*, pp. 104–5.

[46]As examples, see RGIP, vol. 1, pps. 205, 339.

[47]George Kubler, *Mexican Architecture of the Sixteenth Century* (New Haven: Yale University Press, 1948), vol. 1, pp. 47–49; see also Cook and Borah, *Essays*, vol. 3, p. 176.

[48]AGI, Lima, leg. 33, 35, 3 November 1598; Mexico, leg. 22, 4, 128, 6 April 1596; CDHFS, vol. 2, t. 1, p. 46.

[49]Francisco del Paso y Troncoso, *Papeles de Nueva España. Relaciones geográficas de la Diócesis de Michoacán* (Guadalajara: Colección "Siglo XVI," 1958), vol. 1, p. 74.

[50]Francisco del Paso y Troncoso, *Papeles de Nueva España. Relaciones geográficas de la Diócesis de México* (Mexico City: Editorial Cosmos, 1979), pp. 229, 231, 243–45, 258–59, 278.

[51]RGIP, vol. 2, p. 319.

[52]Gibson, *Aztecs*, p. 250.

[53]Garner, "Prices," pp. 285–86.

[54]Woodrow Borah and Sherburne F. Cook, *Price Trends of Some Basic Commodities in Central Mexico, 1531–1570*. Ibero-Americana, 40 (Berkeley and Los Angeles: University of California Press, 1958), p. 48.

[55]Wages and prices from late sixteenth-century Querétaro suggest that textile employees, the poorest-paid workers in the province, earned from twenty to twenty-four reales per month, which was usually enough to buy a total of two bushels of maize, one bushel of wheat, and three lambs. MNAH, Querétaro microfilm series, various years and rolls.

[56]AGI, Mexico, leg. 256, *passim*; RGIP, vol. 2, p. 220; Encinas, *Cedulario*, vol. 4, p. 310.

[57]Gibson, *Aztecs*, p. 218–19; Spalding, *Huarochiri*, pp. 294–301.

[58]CDIRDCO, vol. 9, pp. 386–99; Encinas, *Cedulario*, vol. 1, pp. 181–201.

[59]AGI, Patronato Real, leg. 181, 27, different reports, especially question eight, 1554.

[60]Stern, *Peru*, p. 91.

[61]Quote is from AGI, Lima, leg. 93, report of Núñez de Abendaño, 29 December 1590; Mexico, leg. 19, 1, 21B, 30 January 1559; Mexico leg. 21, 2, 19-J, fol. 3, 24 October 1587; Alonso de Zorita, *Life and Labor in Ancient Mexico*, tr. Benjamin Keen (New Brunswick: Rutgers University Press, 1963), p. 250; Gibson, *Aztecs*, p. 203; Florescano, "Abasto," p. 573.

[62]AGI, Mexico, leg. 70, 21, 21 October 1581; Gibson, *Aztecs*, p. 203.

Chapter Six

[1]Dennis E. Puleston, "The Role of Ramón in Maya Subsistence," and William M. Denevan, "Hydraulic Agriculture in the American Tropics: Forms, Measures, and Recent Research," both in Kent V. Flannery (ed.), *Maya Subsistence: Studies in Memory of Dennis E. Puleston* (New York: Academic Press, 1982), pp. 183, 358–62.

[2]Gonzalo Aguirre Beltrán, "Cultura y nutrición," in *Estudios antropológicos publicados en homenaje al doctor Manuel Gamio* (Mexico City: Universidad Nacional, 1956), p. 230; Richard N. Adams, "Food Habits in Latin America: A Preliminary Historical Survey," in Iago Galdston (ed.), *Human Nutrition: Historic and Scientific* (New York: International Universities Press, 1960), pp. 7–8, 14–16.

[3]Derrick B. Jelliffe and E. F. Patricia Jelliffe, "Field Assessment of Dietary Intake and Nutritional Status," in Nevin S. Scrimshaw and John E. Gordon (eds.), *Malnutrition, Learning, and Behavior* (Cambridge, Mass: MIT Press, 1968), pp. 404–5.

[4]Bernardino de Sahagún, *Historia general de las cosas de Nueva España*, (Mexico City: Editorial Pedro Robredo, 1938), vol. 2, pp. 303–4; Franciso Hernández, *Historia de las plantas de Nueva España* (Mexico City: Imprenta Universitaria, 1942–1946) vol. 3, pp. 869–78.

[5]El Inca Garcilasso de la Vega, *Royal Commentaries of the Incas*, tr. Harold V.

Livermore (Austin: University of Texas Press, 1966), vol. 1, p. 499; anon., *Descripción del virreinato del Perú, crónica inédita de comienzos de siglo XVII* (Rosario: Universidad Nacional del Litoral, 1958), p. 49.

⁶Charles Gibson, *The Aztecs Under Spanish Rule* (Stanford: Stanford University Press, 1964), p. 311.

⁷Murdo J. MacLeod, *Spanish Central America: A Socioeconomic History, 1520–1720* (Berkeley and Los Angeles: University of California Press), p. 215.

⁸The comment of Oscar Lewis that maize contributed from 10 percent to 70 percent of the calories of diets in Tepoztlán is probably a good general statement for central Mexico. Oscar Lewis, *Life in a Mexican Village: Tepoztlán Restudied* (Urbana, Il: University of Illinois Press, 1963), p. 187.

⁹Christopher Columbus, *The Journals and Other Documents of the Life of Christopher Columbus*, tr. Samuel Eliot Morison (New York: Heritage Press, 1963), pp. 65–66.

¹⁰AGN, Cédulas Reales (Originales), vol. 102, 151, 3 June 1773, p. 265.

¹¹R. L. Dressler, "The Pre-Columbian Cultivated Plants of Mexico," *Botanical Museum Leaflets*, Harvard University, 16:6 (1953), pp. 115–72.

¹²Francesco Carletti, *My Voyage Around the World*, tr. Herbert Weinstock (New York: Random House, 1964), p. 62. Jean Andrews discusses the many uses of chiles in *Peppers: The Domesticated Capsicums* (Austin: University of Texas Press, 1984), pp. 72–76.

¹³Motolinía (Toribio de Benavente), *Motolinía's History of the Indians of New Spain*, tr. Elizabeth Andros Foster (Berkeley: The Cortés Society, 1950), p. 222.

¹⁴*Gazetas de México* (Mexico City: Felipe de Zúñiga y Ontiveros, 1784–1809), vol. 1, 21 April 1784, p. 71.

¹⁵Carletti, *Voyage*, p. 54.

¹⁶Pedro Arias de Benavides, *Secretos de Chirurgia* (Valladolid: Francisco Fernández de Cordova, 1567), pp. 40–44.

¹⁷Antonio Vázquez de Espinosa, *Compendium and Description of the West Indies*, tr. Charles Upson Clark (Washington, D.C.: Smithsonian Institution, 1942), p. 370.

¹⁸Gibson, *Aztecs*, pp. 337–45.

¹⁹Motolinía, *Indians*, p. 40.

²⁰Joyce Marcus, "The Plant World of the Sixteenth- and Seventeenth-Century Lowland Maya," in Flannery (ed.), *Maya Subsistence*, pp. 250–51.

²¹Thomas Jeffreys, *The Natural and Civil History of the French Dominions in North and South America* (London: Charing-Cross, 1760), p. 10.

²²José Quintín Olascoaga, *Bromatología de los alimentos industrializados* (Mexico City: n.p., 1963), vol. 3, p. 147.

²³*Ibid*; and Aguirre Beltrán, "Cultura y nutrición," p. 229.

²⁴Sahagún, *Historia*, vol. 3, p. 195; Francisco del Paso y Troncoso, *Relaciones geográficas de la Diócesis de México*, (Mexico City: Editorial Cosmos, 1979), pp. 111, 206, 217.

²⁵Marvin Harris has written a convincing explanation of cannabalism. *Good to Eat: Riddles of Food and Culture* (New York: Simon and Schuster, 1985), pp. 199–234.

²⁶See the scores of references in RGI; Paso y Troncoso, *Diócesis de México*; and his *Papeles de Nueva España: Relaciones geográficas de la Diócesis de Michoacán* (Guadalajara: Coleccion "Siglo XVI," 1958).

²⁷Motolína, *Indians*, p. 224; Sidney W. Mintz, *Sweetness and Power: The Place of Sugar in Modern History* (New York: Viking, 1985), pp. 5–6, 148–49.

²⁸Berta Cabanillas de Rodríguez, *El puertorriqueño y su alimentación a través de su historia: siglos XVI a XIX* (San Juan: Instituto de Cultura Puertorriqueña, 1973), p. 222; ACCM, vol. 6, pp. 191–92, 6 November 1555; vol. 6, pp. 193–95, 11 November 1555; vol. 6, p. 493, 3 October 1561; MNAH, "Visita de obraje de Esteban de Aguilar, 1589," Querétaro microfilm series, rolls 1–2; Luis Chávez Orozco, *Documentos para la historia económica de México* (Mexico City: Publicaciones de la Secretaria de la economia nacional, 1933–1938), vol. 2, p. 57; LCL, vol. 6, pt. 2, p. 352, 7 September 1565; Frederick P. Bowser, *The African Slave in Colonial Peru, 1524–1650* (Stanford: Stanford University Press, 1974), p. 225; Roberto Levillier (ed.), *Gobernantes del Perú. cartas y papeles, siglo XVI* (Madrid: Sucesores de Rivadeneyra, 1921–1926), vol. 8, pp. 404–5; Horacio H. Urteaga (ed.), *Fundación española de Cusco y ordenanzas para su gobierno* (Lima: Talleres Gráficas Sanmarti y Cia, 1926), p. 132.

²⁹AGI, Mexico, leg. 19, 1, 1, 30 June 1536; ACCM, vol. 6, pp. 191–92, 6 November 1555; LCL, vol. 4, p. 492, 12 August 1552; Sherburne F. Cook and Woodrow Borah, *Essays in Population History.* vol. 3, *Mexico and California* (Berkeley and Los Angeles: University of California Press, 1979), p. 174.

³⁰AGI, Lima, 28A, 63 H, fols. 13–14, 15 April 1574; RGIP, vol. 2, p. 323; Ross Hassig, *Trade, Tribute, and Transportation: The Sixteenth-Century Political Economy of the Valley of Mexico* (Norman: University of Oklahoma Press, 1985), pp. 20–21.

³¹AGI, Patronato Real, leg. 187, 14, "Ordenanzas," 8 October 1550 to 21 April 1553; Lima, leg. 28A, 63-H, fols. 13–14, 15 April 1574; Urteaga, *Cusco*, pp. 217–18.

³²Cook and Borah, *Essays*, vol. 3, p. 164; Hassig, *Trade*, pp. 20–21.

³³Cook and Borah, *Essays*, vol. 3, p. 165.

³⁴Fernand Braudel, *Civilization and Capitalism, 15th–18th Century*, vol. 1, *The Structures of Everyday Life*, tr. Siân Reynolds (New York: Harper and Row, 1981), p. 130.

³⁵Most of this evidence is too imprecise to measure the quantity and quality of the diet. For examples, see: MNAH, Nicolás Robles, 23 February 1606, 25 February 1606, Querétaro microfilm series; AGN, General de Parte, vol. 2, 941, fol. 22, 12 August 1580; Hospitales, vol. 77, 1, fols. 64–65, 1 February 1816.

³⁶Motolinía, *Indians*, p. 98.

³⁷Christóbal Méndez, *Book of Bodily Exercise*, tr. Francisco Guerra (New Haven: Elizabeth Licht, 1960), p. 13.

³⁸AGI, Mexico, leg. 70, 2, 26 March 1581.

³⁹Francisco Javier Clavijero, *The History of Mexico*, tr. Charles Cullen (London: G. G. J. & J. Robinson, 1787), vol. 2, p. 357.

⁴⁰Pedro Vicente Cañete y Domíngues, *Guía histórica, geográfica, física, política, civil y legal del gobierno e intendencia de la provincia de Potosí (1787)* (Potosí: Editorial Potosí, 1952), p. 506.

[41]Ignaz Pfefferkorn, *Sonora: A Description of the Province*, tr. Theodore E. Treutlein (Albuquerque: University of New Mexico Press, 1949), p. 195.

[42]RGIP, vol. 1, p. 170.

[43]George Kubler, *Mexican Architecture of the Sixteenth Century* (New Haven: Yale University Press, 1948), vol. 1, p. 46.

[44]RGIP, vol. 1, p. 338; vol. 2, pp. 18, 237; quotation from Paso y Troncoso, *Diócesis de México*, p. 129.

[45]Cook and Borah, *Essays*, vol. 3, pp. 174–75.

[46]*Ibid.*, pp. 173–74, and Woodrow Borah, "Five Centuries of Food Production and Consumption in Central Mexico," manuscript to be published in the *Memoria de la Academia Mexicana de la Historia*, p. 21.

[47]Vázquez de Espinosa, *Compendium*, pp. 480, 482, 733; Keith A. Davies, *Landowners in Colonial Peru* (Austin: University of Texas Press, 1984), p. 91. Nicholas P. Cushner has written the best study of wine production, *Lords of the Land: Sugar, Wine and Jesuit Estates of Coastal Peru, 1600–1767* (Albany: State University of New York Press, 1980).

[48]LCL, vol. 4, p. 126, 10 June 1549.

[49]Jorge Juan and Antonio de Ulloa, *Noticias secretas de America*, (Madrid: Editorial América, 1918), vol. 1, p. 349.

[50]José de Acosta, *Historia natural y moral de las Indias* (Mexico City: Fondo de Cultura Económica, 1940), p. 286; Bernabé Cobo, *Obras* (Madrid: Atlas, 1956), vol. 1, p. 215; Joseph A. Gagliano, "A Social History of Coca" (Ph.D. dissertation, Georgetown University, 1962), pp. 30–56; Nathan Wachtel, "The Indian and the Spanish Conquest," in Leslie Bethell (ed.), *The Cambridge History of Latin America*, vol. 1, *Colonial Latin America* (Cambridge: Cambridge University Press, 1984), p. 229.

[51]RGIP, vol. 1, p. 177; vol. 2, p. 251; Acosta, *Historia*, p. 286; Antonio de León Pinelo, *Questión moral si el chocolate quebranta el ayuno eclesiástico* (Madrid: Juan Gonzales, 1636), pp. 35–36.

[52]ACCM, vol. 5, p. 234, 15 November 1548; vol. 6, p. 327, 2 May 1558; LCL, vol. 4, p. 126, 10 June 1549; Constantino Bayle, "Más sobre abastos en la historia hispanoamerica," *Razón y Fe: Revista Mensual Hispanoamericana*, 50: 639 (1951), pp. 390–91; Michael C. Scardaville, "Crime and the Urban Poor: Mexico City in the Late Colonial Period" (Ph.D. dissertation, Univeristy of Florida, 1977), pp. 209–12.

[53]A. Paredes, "Social Control of Drinking Among the Aztec Indians of Mesoamerica," *Journal of Studies on Alcohol*, 36:9 (September, 1975), pp. 1143–44; Guillermo Calderón Navarez, "Reflections on Alcoholism Among the Prehispanic Peoples of Mexico," *Foreign Psychiatry*, 2:4 (1974), pp. 88–91; C. Morris, "Maize Beer in the Economics, Politics, and Religion of the Inca Empire," in Clifford F. Gastineau, William J. Darby, and Thomas B. Turner, (eds.), *Fermented Food Beverages in Nutrition* (New York: Academic Press, 1979), p. 32.

[54]RGIP, vol. 1, pp. 170, 339; AGI, Lima, leg. 28A, 10 June 1570.

[55]Benjamin Keen mentions the opinion shared by many of the great chroniclers of the sixteenth century—Motolonía, Durán, Sahagún—that Indians drank more after the conquest than before. Some earlier writers, such as Bernal Díaz del Castillo, emphasized the pervasiveness of pre-conquest drinking, perhaps to justify

the conquest. *The Aztec Image in Western Thought* (New Brunswick, NJ: Rutgers University Press, 1971), pp. 63, 101, 111, 117, 121, 125.

[56]RGIP, vol. 1, pp. 377–80.

[57]Cañete y Domíngues, *Guía*, p. 42.

[58]Scardaville, "Crime," pp. 209–12.

[59]Juan Roca and Roberto Llamas, "Consideraciones sobre el valor alimenticio del pulque," *Anales del Instituto de Biología*, 10:1–2 (March–June, 1939), p. 370.

[60]Richmond K. Anderson, José Calvo, Gloria Serrano, and George C. Payne, "A Study of the Nutritional Food Habits of Otomí Indians in the Mesquital Valley of Mexico," *American Journal of Public Health and the Nation's Health*, 36:8 (August, 1946), p. 888.

[61]C.S.L. Davies, "Les rations alimentaires de l'armée et de la marine anglaise au XVIe siècle," *Annales, E.S.C.* 18:1 (January–February, 1963), p. 139; Michel Morineau, "Rations de marine (Angleterre, Hollande, Suède et Russie)," *Annales, E.S.C.*, 20:6 (November–December, 1965), pp. 1150–53; John C. Super, "Spanish Diet in the Atlantic Crossing, the 1570s," *Terrae Incognitae*, 16 (1984), p. 62.

[62]Braudel, *Civilization,* vol. 1, pp. 231–49.

[63]Missionary manuals recommended that friars ask specific questions about Indian drinking practices. Juan Baptista, *Confessionario en lengua mexicana y castellana* (Santiago Tlatilulco: Melchior Ocharte, 1599), p. 56; CDIRDCO, vol. 9, p. 433; Encinas, *Cedulario*, vol. 4, pp. 348–49; Juan de Solórzano y Pereyra, *Política Indiana* (Madrid: Compañía Ibero-Americana de Publicaciones, 1930), vol. 1, pp. 383–93; John Howland Rowe, "Inca Culture at the Time of the Spanish Conquest," in Julian H. Steward (ed.), *Handbook of South American Indians: The Andean Civilizations* (Washington: Smithsonian Institution, 1946), vol. 2, p. 292.

[64]ENE, vol. 4, p. 77.

[65]William B. Taylor, *Drinking, Homicide, and Rebellion in Colonial Mexican Villages* (Stanford: Stanford University Press, 1979), pp. 44–47.

[66]Oswaldo Gonçalves de Lima, *El Maguey y el pulque en los codices mexicanos* (Mexico City: Fondo de Cultura Económica, 1956), p. 55; Mario C. Vázquez, "La chicha en los paises andinos," *América Indígena*, 27 (1967), p. 273.

[67]Luis Capoche, *Relación general de la Villa Imperial de Potosí* (Madrid: Atlas, 1959), p. 141; MNAH, Juan Dalava Ybarra, 9 November 1589, Querétaro microfilm series, roll 21.

[68]Gibson, *Aztecs*, p. 409. Others have also emphasized the significance of widespread and persistant alcohol use by Indians. For example, see Wachtel, "Indian," pp. 228–229.

[69]Donald J. Horton, "The Functions of Alcohol in Primitive Societies," *Quarterly Journal of Studies on Alcohol*, 4 (1943), pp. 216–30, *passim.*

[70]For a review of some of the arguments Peter B. Field, "A New Cross-cultural Study of Drunkenness," in David J. Pittman and Charles R. Snyder (eds.), *Society, Culture and Drinking Patterns* (New York: John Wiley and Sons, 1962), pp. 48–72, *passim.*

[71]Fidel de Lejarza, "Las borracheras y el problema de las conversiones en Indias," *Archivo Ibero-Americano*, 1 (1941), p. 115.

[72]D. L. Fenna *et al.*, "Ethanol Metabolism in Various Racial Groups," in

Michael W. Everett, Jack O. Waddell, and Dwight B. Heath (eds.), *Cross-cultural Approaches to the Study of Alcohol: An Interdisciplinary Perspective* (The Hague: Mouton, 1976), p. 234; Lynn J. Bennon and Ting-Kai Li, "Alcohol Metabolism in American Indians and Whites," *The New England Journal of Medicine*, 294:1 (January, 1976), pp. 9–13.

[73]Scardaville, "Crime," pp. 209–10.

[74]Gonzalo Fernández de Oviedo, *Sumario de la natural historia de las Indias* (Mexico City: Fondo de Cultura Económica, 1950), p. 133.

[75]Carletti, *Voyage*, p. 44.

[76]Jorge Juan and Antonio de Ulloa, *A Voyage to South America*, tr. John Adams (London: L. Davis, 1772), vol. 1, p. 289. Cañete y Domínguez has a similar statement on the Indians of Potosí. *Guía histórica*, p. 412.

[77]José Hipólito Unanue, *Observaciones sobre el clima de Lima...* (Lima: Imp. Lux, 1940), p. 78.

[78]RLI, Lib. 6, Tit. 1, Ley, 37 (vol. 2, pp. 197–98).

[79]*Diario de México*, vol. 13, pp. 514–15.

[80]Roca and Llamas, "Consideraciones," p. 368; Anderson, "Otomí," p. 888; W-T. Leung, *Food Composition Table for Use in Latin America* (Washington, D.C.: U.S. Government Printing Office, 1961), p. 91.

[81]Jorge Bejarano, *La derrota de un vicio: orígen e historia de la chicha* (Bogotá: Editorial Iqueima, 1950), pp. 90–91.

[82]Braudel, *Civilization*, vol. 1, p. 261.

Chapter Seven

[1]Pierre Chaunu, *European Expansion in the Later Middle Ages*, tr. Katharine Bertram (Amsterdam: North-Holland Publishing Company, 1969), pp. 283–88; see also Immanuel Wallerstein, *The Modern World-System: Capitalist Agriculture and the Origins of the European World-Economy in the Sixteenth Century* (New York: Academic Press, 1974), pp. 42–44.

[2]Bartolomé de las Casas, *Historia de las Indias* (Mexico City: Fondo de Cultura Económica, 1951), vol. 3, p. 37; CVD, vol. 3, pp. 359, 382, 385.

[3]As examples, see PNV, vol. 7, pp. 109, 118, 140–43; *Actas del Cabildo de Guayaquil* (Guayaquil: Publicaciones del Archivo Histórico del Guayas, 1972–1973, vol. 1, pp. 199, 253.

[4]*CDIRDCO*, vol. 11, pp. 48–49.

[5]Edmund S. Morgan, *American Slavery, American Freedom. The Ordeal of Colonial Virginia* (New York: W. W. Norton, 1975), pp. 71–92.

[6]Maximilien Sorre, *Les fondements biologiques de la géographie humaine: essai d'une écologie de l'homme* (Paris: A. Colin, 1971), p. 275–81.

[7]Fernand Braudel, *Civilization and Capitalism, 15th–18th Century*, vol. 1, *The Structures of Everyday Life*, tr. Siân Reynolds (New York: Harper and Row, 1981), p. 74.

[8]*Ibid.*

[9]*Ibid.*, p. 76.

[10]*Ibid.*, p. 74; W. L. Langer, "American Foods and Europe's Population Growth, 1750–1850," *Journal of Social History*, 9 (Winter, 1975), pp. 51–66.

[11]J. H. Parry, *The Age of Reconnaissance* (New York: Mentor Books, 1964), p. 53; Fernand Braudel, *Capitalism and Material Life*, tr. Miriam Kochan (New York: Harper and Row, 1973), vol. 1, pp. 570–606; Wallerstein, *Modern World*, pp. 217–19.

[12]Fernand Braudel, *The Mediterranean and the Mediterranean World in the Age of Philip II*, tr. Siân Reynolds (New York: Harper and Row), vol. 1, p. 573.

[13]Jaime Vicens Vives, *An Economic History of Spain*, tr. Frances M. López-Morillas (Princeton: Princeton University Press, 1969), p. 461.

[14]Thomas Trapham, *A Discourse of the State of Health in the Island of Jamaica . . .* (London: R. Boulter, 1679), pp. 52–67; Thomas Tryon, *Friendly Advice to the Gentlemen-Planters of the East and West Indies* (London: Andrew Soule, 1684), pp. 49–53; Richard S. Dunn, *Sugar and Slaves* (Chapel Hill: University of North Carolina Press, 1972), p. 275–81.

[15]Thales de Azevedo, *Povoamento da Cidade do Salvador* (São Paulo: Companhia Editôra Nacional, 1955), pp. 378–388.

[16]Richard N. Adams, "Food Habits in Latin America: A Preliminary Historical Survey," in Iago Galdston (ed.), *Human Nutrition: Historic and Scientific* (New York: International Universities Press, 1960), p. 9.

[17]AGN, Alhóndigas y Pósitos, vol. 4, 1, fols. 139–144, 26 March 1793. Some of the cheap bread, however, was so bad that it should "usually just be bought for dogs." AGN, Historia, vol. 135, fols. 81v.–82, 17 April 1793.

[18]*Gazetas de México* (Mexico City: Manuel Antonio Valdés, 1784–1809), vol. 11, p. 273, 15 April 1803. AGN, Hospitales, vol. 9, 5, fols. 79–81, 27 November 1809; fols. 87–89, 19 December 1809.

[19]Louis Stouff, *Ravitaillement et alimentation en Provence aux 14e et 15e siècles* (Paris: Mouton, 1970), pp. 249–50; Hugues Neveux, "L'alimentation du XIVe au XVIIIe siècle," *Revue d' Histoire Economique et Sociale*, 61 (1973), p. 358.

[20]AGN, Cédulas Reales, Originales, vol. 99, fols. 166–268, *passim*.

[21]LCL, vol. 12, "Ordenanzas hechas por el Virrey Don García Hurtado de Mendoza, pp. 673–79, 24 January 1594; AGI, Mexico, leg. 2779, "Ordenanzas de la Fiel Ejecutoría, 1728", p. 22.

[22]Woodrow Borah, *New Spain's Century of Depression*, Ibero-Americana, 35 (Berkeley and Los Angeles: University of California Press, 1951), p. 22.

[23]*Ibid.*, p. 26.

[24]P. J. Bakewell, *Silver Mining and Society in Colonial Mexico: Zacatecas, 1546–1700* (Cambridge: The University Press, 1971), pp. 223–28.

[25]Woodrow Borah and Sherburne F. Cook, *Price Trends of Some Basic Commodities in Central Mexico, 1531–1579*, Ibero-Americana, 40 (Berkeley and Los Angeles: University of California Press, 1958), p. 49.

[26]Bakewell, *Silver Mining*, p. 230.

[27]Vicens Vives, *Economic History*, p. 393.

[28]Murdo J. MacLeod, *Spanish Central America: A Socioeconomic History,*

1520–1720 (Berkeley and Los Angeles: University of California Press, 1973), p. 204.

²⁹*Ibid.*, pp. 209–20.

³⁰Karen Spalding, *Huarochiri: An Andean Society Under Inca and Spanish Rule* (Palo Alto: Stanford University Press, 1984), pp. 134–35; Jeffrey A. Cole, *The Potosí Mita, 1573–1700* (Palo Alto: Stanford University Press, 1985), pp. 24, 30; Steve J. Stern, *Peru's Indian Peoples and the Challenge of Spanish Conquest* (Madison: The University of Wisconsin Press, 1982), pp. 140–55.

³¹Braudel, *Civilization*, vol. 1, p. 75. Emmanuel Le Roy Ladurie describes the many and tragic consequences of subsistence crises in sixteenth-century France. *The Peasants of Languedoc*, tr. John Day (Urbana, IL: University of Illinois Press, 1974).

³²This observation is based on sixteenth-century records of LCL and ACCM.

³³Murdo MacLeod, "Aspects of the Internal Economy of Colonial Spanish America: Labour; Taxation; Distribution and Exchange," in Leslie Bethell (ed.), *The Cambridge History of Latin America*. vol. 2, *Colonial Latin America* (Cambridge: Cambridge University Press, 1984), p. 231; Nathan Wachtel, "The Indian and the Spanish Conquest," in vol. 1 of the same series, pp. 207–248, *passim*; George Kubler, "The Quechua in the Colonial World," in Julian H. Steward (ed.), *Handbook of South American Indians: The Andean Civilizations* (Washington, D.C.: Smithsonian Institution Bureau of American Ethnology, 1946), vol. 2, pp. 364–70; Stern, *Peru's Indians*, pp. 90–91, 148–55.

Bibliography

Food is a topic of such scope that the evidence for studying it is almost inexhaustible. Royal decrees and laws define the nature of imperial agricultural and nutritional interests; *cabildo* and guild deliberations illustrate the complexity of food politics at the local level; tithe, taxation, and commercial records yield information on production and distribution; *materia medica* help to understand contemporary perceptions of nutrition and food; chroniclers and other first-hand observers describe everything from the quantity of food available to its cultural significance. My intent was to sample as much of this evidence as feasible in the hopes of arriving at some assessment of the significance of food supplies in the sixteenth century. The following bibliography refers only to those materials cited in the text.

Manuscript Archives

Archivo General de Indias (AGI), Seville
   Contaduría
   Contratación
   Indiferente General

Lima
Mexico
Patronato Real
Quito

Archivo General de la Nación (AGN), Mexico City
Alhóndigas y Pósitos
Cédulas Reales, Originales
Historia
Hospitales

Biblioteca Nacional, Mexico City
Gabinete de Manuscritos

Museo Nacional de Antopología e Historia (MNAH), Mexico City
Querétaro Microfilm Series

Printed Sources

Abbeville, Claude D. *Histoire de la mission des Pères Capucins en l'Isle de Maragnan . . .* Paris: Imprimerie de François Huby, 1614.
Acosta, José de. *Historia natural y moral de las Indias.* Mexico City: Fondo de Cultura Económica, 1940.
Actas Capitulares del Ayuntamiento de la Habana. Ed. Emilio Roig de Leuchsenring. 2 vols. Havana: Municipio de la Havana, 1937.
Actas de cabildo de la ciudad de Mexico. 50 volumes. Mexico City: Ignacio Bejarano, 1889–1916.
Actas del Cabildo de Guayaquil. 3 vols. Guayaquil: Publicaciones del Archivo Histórico del Guayas, 1972–73.
Adams, Richard N. "Food Habits in Latin America: A Preliminary Historical Survey." In Iago Galdston (ed.). *Human Nutrition: Historic and Scientific.* New York: International Universities Press, 1960, pp. 1–22.
Aguirre Beltrán, Gonzalo. "Cultura y nutrición." In *Estudios antropológicos publicados en homenaje al doctor Manuel Gamio.* Mexico City: Universidad Nacional, 1956, pp. 227–49.
Altamira y Crevea, Rafael, *et al. Contribuciones a la historia municipal de América.* Mexico City: Instituto Panamericano de Geografía e Historia, 1951.
Altman, Ida, and James Lockhart (eds.). *Provinces of Early Mexico.* Los Angeles: UCLA Latin American Center Publications, 1976.
Alvarez Ossorio y Redín, Miguel. *Con estos dos memoriales, se descubren medios para quitar los tributos y sustentar continuamente quatro millones de personas pobres.* Madrid: n.p., 1686.
———. *Discurso universal de las causas que ofenden esta monarquía, y remedios eficaces para todas.* Madrid: n.p., 1686.
Alzate y Ramírez, José Antonio. *Consejos útiles para socorrer a la necesidad en tiempo que escasen los comestibles.* Mexico City: Felipe de Zúñiga y Ontiveros, 1786.

Anderson, Richmond K., José Calvo, Gloria Serrano, and George C. Payne. "A Study of the Nutritional Food Habits of Otomí Indians in the Mesquital Valley of Mexico." *American Journal of Public Health and the Nation's Health*, 36:8 (August 1946), pp. 883–903.

Andrews, Jean. *Peppers: The Domesticated Capsicums*. Austin: University of Texas Press, 1984.

Anon. *Descripción del Virreinato del Perú: Crónica inédita de comienzos de siglo XVII*. Rosario: Universidad Nacional del Litoral, 1958.

Appleby, A. B. "Famine, Mortality, and Epidemic Disease: A Comment." *Economic History Review*, 30 (1977), pp. 508–12.

————. "Nutrition and Disease: The Case of London, 1550–1756." *Journal of Interdisciplinary History*, 6:1 (Summer, 1975), pp. 1–22.

"Aranzel de los jornales que se han de pagar a los indios." Lima: n.p., 1687.

Arias de Benavides, Pedro. *Secretos de chirurgia, especial de las enfermedades de morbo gálico . . .* Valladolid: Francisco Fernández de Cordova, 1567.

Ashtor, Eliyahu. "An Essay on the Diet of the Various Classes in the Medieval Levant." In Robert Forster and Orest Ranum (eds.). *Biology of Man in History*. Baltimore: Johns Hopkins University Press, 1975, pp. 125–62.

Atúnez de Mayolo R., Santiago. "La nutrición en el antiguo Perú." In III Congreso Peruano. *El hombre y la cultura andina*. Lima: Ramiro Matos M., 1977, vol. 5, 811–28.

Aymard, M. "Pour l'histoire de l'alimentation: quelques remarques de méthode." *Annales. E.S.C.*, 30 (1975), pp. 431–44.

Azara, Félix de. *Memoria sobre el estado rural del Río de la Plata y otros informes*. Buenos Aires: Editorial Bajel, 1942.

Azevedo, Thales de. *Povoamento da Cidade do Salvador*. 2d. ed. Sâo Paulo: Companhia Editôra Nacional, 1955.

Bakewell, Peter. *Miners of the Red Mountain: Indian Labor in Potosí, 1545–1650*. Albuquerque: University of New Mexico Press, 1984.

————. "Mining in Colonial Spanish America." In Leslie Bethell (ed.). *The Cambridge History of Latin America. Colonial Latin America*. Cambridge: Cambridge University Press, 1984, vol. 1, pp. 105–52.

————. *Silver Mining and Society in Colonial Mexico: Zacatecas, 1546–1700*. Cambridge: The University Press, 1971.

Barrett, Ward. "The Meat Supply of Colonial Cuernavaca." *Annals of the Association of American Geographers*, 64:4 (December, 1974), pp. 525–40.

Bayle, Constantino, S. J. "Más sobre abastos en la historia hispanoamericano." *Razón y Fe: Revista Mensual Hispanoamericana*, 50: 639 (1951), pp. 388–403.

————."Nuevo capítulo de abastos en la América española. *Razón y Fe: Revista Mensual Hispanoamerica*, 50: 632–33 (1950), pp. 274–85.

Bejarano, Jorge. *La derrota de un vicio: origen e historia de la chicha*. Bogotá: Editorial Iqueima, 1950.

Bennett, M. K. "Famine." *International Encyclopedia of the Social Sciences*. New York: The Macmillan Company and the Free Press, 1968, vol. 5, pp. 322–26.

Bennon, Lynn J. and Ting-Kai Li. "Alcohol Metabolism in American Indians and Whites." *The New England Journal of Medicine*, 294: 1 (January, 1976), pp. 9–13.

Bergman, Roland. "Subsistence Agriculture in Latin America." In John C. Super and Thomas C. Wright (eds.). *Food, Politics, and Society in Latin America.* Lincoln: University of Nebraska Press, 1985, pp. 106–132.

Bethell, Leslie (ed.). *The Cambridge History of Latin America.* Vols. 1 and 2. *Colonial Latin America.* Cambridge: Cambridge University Press, 1984.

Boemus, Johann. *El libro de las costumbres de todas las gentes del mundo, y de las Indias.* Tr. Francisco Thamara. Anvers: Martin Nucio, 1556.

Borah, Woodrow. "Five Centuries of Food Production and Consumption in Central Mexico." To be published in *Memoria de la Academia Mexicana de la Historia.*

———. *New Spain's Century of Depression.* Ibero-Americana, 35. Berkeley and Los Angeles: University of California Press, 1951.

———. and Sherburne F. Cook. *Price Trends of Some Basic Commodities in Central Mexico, 1531–1570.* Ibero-Americana, 40. Berkeley and Los Angeles: University of California Press, 1958.

Bowser, Frederick P. *The African Slave in Colonial Peru, 1524–1650.* Stanford: Stanford University Press, 1974.

Boxer, Charles R. *The Golden Age of Brazil, 1695–1750.* Berkeley and Los Angeles: University of California Press, 1964.

Brading, David A. *Haciendas and Ranchos in the Mexican Bajío: León, 1700–1860.* Cambridge: Cambridge University Press, 1978.

Braudel, Fernand. *Capitalism and Material Life.* Tr. Miriam Kochan. 2 vols. New York: Harper and Row, 1973.

———. *Civilization and Capitalism, 15th–18th Century.* Vol. 1. *The Structures of Everyday Life.* Tr. Siân Reynolds. New York: Harper and Row, 1981.

———. *The Mediterranean and the Mediterranean World in the Age of Philip II.* Tr. Siân Reynolds. 2 vols. New York: Harper and Row, 1975.

Bustamante, Miguel E. "Aspectos históricos y epidemiológicos del hambre en México." In Enrique Florescano y Elsa Malvido (comps.). *Ensayo sobre la historia de las epidemias en Mexico.* Mexico City: Instituto Mexicano del Seguro Social, 1982, vol. 1, pp. 37–66.

Cabanillas de Rodríguez, Berta. *El puertorriqueño y su alimentación a través de su historia: siglos XVI a XIX.* San Juan: Instituto de Cultura Puertorriqueña, 1973.

Calderón Navarez, Guillermo. "Reflections on Alcoholism Among the Prehispanic Peoples of Mexico." *Foreign Psychiatry,* 2:4 (1974), pp. 78–92.

Cañete y Domínguez, Pedro Vicente. *Guía histórico, geográfica, física, política, civil y legal del gobierno e intendencia de la provincia de Potosí (1787).* Potosí: Editoral Potosí, 1952.

Capoche, Luis. *Relación general de la Villa Imperial de Potosí.* Madrid: Ediciones Atlas, 1959.

Carcer y Disdier, Mariano de. *Apuntes para la historia de la transculturación Indoespañola.* Mexico City: Instituto de Historia, 1953.

Carletti, Francesco. *My Voyage Around the World.* Tr. Herbert Weinstock. New York: Random House, 1964.

Carrío de la Vandera, Alonso. *El Lazarillo de Ciegos Caminantes.* Barcelona: Editorial Labor, 1973.

Casas, Bartolomé de las. *Historia de las Indias.* 3 vols. Mexico City: Fondo de Cultura Económica, 1951.

Castro, Josué de. *The Geography of Hunger.* Boston: Little, Brown and Co., 1951.

Chang, K. C. (ed.). *Food in Chinese Culture: Anthropological and Historical Perspectives.* New Haven: Yale University Press, 1977.

Chaunu, Pierre. *European Expansion in the Later Middle Ages.* Tr. Katharine Bertram. Amsterdam and New York: North-Holland Publishing Co., 1979.

Chávez Orozco, Luis. *Documentos para la historia económica de México.* 12 vols. Mexico City: Publicaciones de la Secretaría de la Economía Nacional, 1933–1938.

Chevalier, François. *La formation des grands domaines au Mexique.* Paris: Institut d'Ethnologie, 1952.

Cieza de León, Pedro de. *La crónica del Perú.* Madrid: Espasa-Calpe, 1962.

Clavijero, Francisco Javier. *The History of Mexico.* Tr. Charles Cullen. 2 vols. London: G.G.J. & J. Robinson, 1787.

Cobo, Bernabé. *Obras.* 2 vols. Madrid: Ediciones Atlas, 1956.

Cole, Jeffrey A. *The Potosí Mita, 1573–1700.* Palo Alto: Stanford University Press, 1985.

Colección de documentos inéditos para la historia de España. Ed. Martín Fernández Navarrete *et al.* 112 vols. New York: Kraus Reprints, 1964.

Colección de documentos para la historia de la formación social de Hispanoamérica, 1493–1810. Ed. Richard Konetzke. 3 vols. in 5. Madrid: Consejo Superior de Investigaciones Científicas, 1953.

Colección de los viages y descubrimientos que hicieron por mar los Españoles desde fines del siglo XV. Ed. Martín Fernández de Navarrete. 5 vols. Buenos Aires: Editorial Guarania, 1945.

Columbus, Christopher. *Journals and Other Documents on the Life and Voyages of Christopher Columbus.* Tr. Samuel Eliot Morison. New York: The Heritage Press, 1963.

Cook, David Noble. *Demographic Collapse: Indian Peru, 1520–1620.* Cambridge: Cambridge University Press, 1981.

Cook, Sherburne F., and Woodrow Borah. *Essays in Population History.* Vol. 3. *Mexico and California.* Berkeley and Los Angeles: University of California Press, 1979.

———. "The Rate of Population Change in Central Mexico, 1550–1570." *Hispanic American Historical Review,* 37:4 (November, 1957), pp. 463–70.

Cortés, Hernán. *Cartas de relación de la conquista de Méjico.* 2 vols. Madrid: Espasa-Calpe, 1942.

Cravioto, René O. "Valor nutritivo de los alimentos mexicanos." *América Indígena,* 11:4 (October, 1951), pp. 297–311.

Crosby, Alfred, W. Jr. *The Columbian Exchange.* Westport, CT: Greenwood Press, 1972.

Cross, Harry. "Living Standards in Rural Nineteenth-Century Mexico: Zacatecas, 1820–1880." *Journal of Latin American Studies,* 10:1 (May, 1978), pp. 1–19.

Cummings, Richard Osborn. *The American and His Food. A History of Food Habits in the United States.* Chicago: University of Chicago Press, 1941.

Cushner, Nicholas P. *Lords of the Land: Sugar, Wine and Jesuit Estates of Coastal Peru, 1600–1767*. Albany: State University of New York Press, 1980.

Davies, C. S. L. "Les rations alimentaires de l'armée et de la marine anglaise au XVIᵉ siècle." *Annales, E.S.C.*, 18:1 (January–February, 1963), pp. 139–41.

Davies, Keith A. *Landowners in Colonial Peru*. Austin: University of Texas Press, 1984.

Denevan, William M. "The Aboriginal Population of Amazonia." In William M. Denevan (ed.). *The Native Population of the Americas in 1492*. Madison: University of Wisconsin Press, 1976, pp. 205–34.

———. "Hydraulic Agriculture in the American Tropics: Forms, Measures, and Recent Research." In Kent V. Flannery (ed.). *Maya Subsistence: Studies in Memory of Dennis E. Puleston*. New York: Academic Press, 1982.

———. (ed.). *The Native Population of the Americas in 1492*. Madison: University of Wisconsin Press, 1976.

Diario de México. 15 vols. Mexico City: Imprenta de Doña María Fernández Jáuregui, 1805–1811.

Díaz del Castillo, Bernal. *The Discovery and Conquest of Mexico*. Tr. A.P. Maudslay. New York: Farrar, Straus, and Cudahy, 1956.

Dobrizhoffer, Martin. *An Account of the Abipones, an Equestrian People of Paraguay*. Tr. Sarah Henry Coleridge. 3 vols. London: John Murray, 1822.

Domínguez y Compañy, Francisco. "Funciones económicas del cabildo colonial hispano-americano." In Rafael Altamira y Crevea *et al. Contribuciones a la historia municipal de América*. Mexico City: Instituto Panamericano de Geografía e Historia, 1951.

Dressler, R. L. "The Pre-Columbian Cultivated Plants of Mexico." *Botanical Museum Leaflets* (Harvard University), 16:6 (1953), pp. 115–72.

Drummond, J. C., and Anne Wilbraham. *The Englishman's Food: A History of Five Centuries of English Diet*. Oxford: Alden Press, 1939.

Dunn, Richard S. *Sugar and Slaves*. Chapel Hill: University of North Carolina Press, 1972.

Du Tertre, Jean Baptiste. *Histoire générale des Isles des Christophe . . .* Paris: Chez Jacques Langlois, 1640.

Encinas, Diego de. *Cedulario Indiano*. 4 vols. Madrid: Ediciones Cultura Hispánica, 1945.

Everett, Michael W., Jack O. Waddell, and Dwight B. Heath (eds.). *Cross-cultural Approaches to the Study of Alcohol: An Interdisciplinary Perspective*. The Hague: Mouton, 1976.

Farriss, Nancy M. *Maya Society Under Colonial Rule: The Collective Enterprise of Survival*. Princeton: Princeton University Press, 1984.

Fenna, D., *et al.* "Ethanol Metabolism in Various Racial Groups." In Michael Everett, Jack O. Waddell, and Dwight B. Heath (eds.). *Cross-cultural Approaches to the Study of Alcohol: An Interdisciplinary Perspective*. The Hague: Mouton, 1976, pp. 227–34.

Fernández de Oviedo, Gonzalo. *Sumario de la natural historia de las Indias*. Mexico City: Fondo de Cultura Económica, 1950.

Field, Peter B. "A New Cross-cultural Study of Drunkenness." In David J. Pittman and Charles R. Snyder (eds.). *Society, Culture and Drinking Patterns.* New York: John Wiley and Sons, 1962, pp. 48–74.

Flannery, Kent V. (ed.). *Maya Subsistence: Studies in Memory of Dennis E. Puleston.* New York: Academic Press, 1982.

Florescano, Enrique. "El abasto y la legislación de granos en el siglo XVI." *Historia Mexicana,* 14:4 (April–June, 1965), pp. 567–630.

————. "The Formation and Economic Structure of the Hacienda in New Spain." In Leslie Bethell (ed). *The Cambridge History of Latin America. Colonial Latin America.* Cambridge: Cambridge University Press, 1984, vol. 2, pp. 153–88.

————. *Precios del maíz y crisis agrícolas en Mexico (1708–1810).* Mexico City: El Colegio de Mexico, 1969.

————. and Elsa Malvido (comps.). *Ensayos sobre la historia de las epidemias en México.* 2 vols. Mexico City: Instituto Mexicano del Seguro Social, 1982.

Forster, Robert, and Orest Ranum (eds.). *Biology of Man in History.* Baltimore: Johns Hopkins University Press, 1975.

Gagliano, Joseph A. "A Social History of Coca." Ph.D. dissertation. Georgetown University, 1962.

Galloway, J. H. "Agricultural Reform and the Enlightenment in Late Colonial Brazil." *Agricultural History,* 53:4 (October, 1979), pp. 763–79.

Garcilaso de la Vega, el Inca. *Royal Commentaries of the Incas.* Tr. Harold V. Livermore. 2 vols. Austin: University of Texas Press, 1966.

Garner, Richard L. "Price Trends in Eighteenth-Century Mexico." *Hispanic American Historical Review,* 65:2 (May, 1985), pp. 279–325.

Gastineau, Clifford F., William J. Darby, and Thomas B. Turner (eds.). *Fermented Food Beverages in Nutrition.* New York. Academic Press, 1979.

Gazetas de México. 16 vols. Mexico City: Felipe de Zúñga y Ontiveros, 1784–1809.

Gentil da Silva, José. *Desarrollo económico, subsistencia y decadencia en España.* Madrid: Editorial Ciencia Nueva, 1967.

Gerard, John. *The Herball, or Generall Histories of Plantes.* London: Norton, 1597.

Gibson, Charles. *The Aztecs Under Spanish Rule.* Stanford: Stanford University Press, 1964.

————. *Tlaxcala in the Sixteenth Century.* Stanford ed. Stanford: Stanford University Press, 1967.

Gonçales de Lima, Oswaldo. *El Maguey y el pulque en los códices Mexicanos.* Mexico City: Fondo de Cultura Económica, 1956.

Gongora, Mario. *Studies in the Colonial History of Spanish America.* London and New York: Cambridge University Press, 1975.

Guerra y Sánchez, Ramiro. *Sugar and Society in the Caribbean: An Economic History of Cuban Agriculture.* New Haven: Yale University Press, 1964.

Hakluyt, Richard (ed.). *The Principal Navigations, Voyages, Traffiques and Discoveries of the English Nation.* 8 vols. London and Toronto: J. M. Dent, 1927–28.

Hamilton, Earl J. "Wages and Subsistence on Spanish Treasure Ships." *Journal of Political Economy,* 37 (1929), pp. 430–50.

Harris, Marvin. *Cows, Pigs, Wars and Witches: The Riddles of Culture.* New York: Vintage Books, 1978.

————. *Good to Eat: Riddles of Food and Culture*. New York: Simon and Schuster, 1985.

Hassig, Ross. "The Famine of One Rabbit: Ecological Causes and Social Consequences of a Precolumbian Calamity." *Journal of Anthropological Research*, 37:2 (Spring, 1981), pp. 172–82.

————. *Trade, Tribute, and Transportation: The Sixteenth-Century Political Economy of the Valley of Mexico*. Norman: University of Oklahoma Press, 1985.

Heckscher, Eli F. *An Economic History of Sweden*. Cambridge, MA: Harvard University Press, 1954.

Hernández, Francisco. *Historia de las plantas de Nueva España*. 3 vols. Mexico City: Imprenta Universitaria, 1942–46.

Hernández Rodríguez, Rosaura. "Epidemias y calamidades en el México prehispánico." In Enrique Florescano and Elsa Malvido (comps.). *Ensayos sobre la historia de las epidemias en México*. Mexico City: Instituto Mexicano del Seguro Social, 1982, vol. 1, pp. 139–56.

Hufton, Olwen. "Social Conflict and the Grain Supply in Eighteenth-Century France." *Journal of Interdisciplinary History*, 14:2 (August, 1983), pp. 303–31.

Humboldt, Alejandro de. *Ensayo político sobre el Reino de la Nueva España*. Tr. Vito Alessio Robles. 5 vols. Mexico City: Editorial Pedro Robredo, 1941.

————. *Personal Narrative of Travels to the Equinoctial Regions of America During the Years 1799–1804*. Tr. Homasina Ross. 3 vols. London: Henry G. Bohn, 1852.

Jeffreys, Thomas. *The Natural and Civil History of the French Dominions in North and South America*. London: Charing-Cross, 1760.

Jelliffe, Derrick B. and E. F. Patricia Jelliffe. "Field Assessment of Dietary Intake and Nutritional Status." In Nevin S. Scrimshaw and J. E. Gordon (eds.). *Malnutrition, Learning, and Behavior*. Cambridge, MA: MIT Press, 1968, pp. 397–409.

Jiménez, Francisco. *Quatro libros de la naturaleza*. Mexico City: Oficina de la Secretaría de Fomento, 1880.

Jiménez de la Espada, Marcos (ed.). *Relaciones geográficas de Indias: Perú*. 3 vols. Madrid: Ediciones Atlas, 1965.

Juan, Jorge, and Antonio de Ulloa. *Noticias Secretas de América*. 2 vols. Madrid: Editorial América, 1918.

————. *A Voyage to South America*. Tr. John Adams. 2 vols. London: L. Davis, 1772.

Kaplan, Steven L. *Bread, Politics and Political Economy in the Reign of Louis XV*. 2 vols. The Hague: Martinus Nijhoff, 1976.

Keen, Benjamin. *The Aztec Image in Western Thought*. New Brunswick: Rutgers University Press, 1971.

Keith, Robert G. *Conquest and Agrarian Change: The Emergence of the Hacienda System on the Peruvian Coast*. Cambridge: Harvard University Press, 1976.

Kubler, George. *Mexican Architecture of the Sixteenth Century*. 2 vols. New Haven: Yale University Press, 1948.

————. "The Quechua in the Colonial World." In Julian H. Steward (ed.). *Handbook of South American Indians: The Andean Civilizations*. Washington, D.C.: Smithsonian Institution, 1946, vol. 2, pp. 331–410.

Laet, Joannes de. *L'Histoire du Nouveau Monde* . . . . Leyde: Chez Bonaventure, 1640.

Langer, W. L. "American Foods and Europe's Population Growth, 1750–1850." *Journal of Social History*, 9 (Winter, 1975), pp. 51–66.

Lejarza, Fidel de. "Las borracheras y el problema de las conversiones en Indias." *Archivo Ibero-Americano*, 1 (1941), pp. 111–42.

León Pinelo, Antonio de. *Questión moral si el chocolate quebranta el ayuno eclesiástico.* . . . Madrid: Juan González, 1636.

Le Roy Ladurie, Emmanuel. *The Peasants of Languedoc.* Tr. John Day. Urbana, Il: University of Illinois Press, 1974.

Leung, W.-T. *Food Composition Table for Use in Latin America.* Washington, D.C.: U.S. Government Printing Office, 1961.

Levillier, Roberto (ed.). *Gobernantes del Perú: Cartas y papeles, siglo XVI.* 14 vols. Madrid: Sucesores de Rivadeneyra, 1921–26.

Lewis, Oscar. *Life in a Mexican Village: Tepoztlán Restudied.* Urbana, IL: University of Illinois Press, 1963.

Libro de las bulas y pragmáticas de los Reyes Católicos. 2 vols. Madrid: Instituto de España, 1973.

Libros de cabildos de Lima: 1534–1611. 16 vols. Lima: Torres Aguirre, 1935–48.

Linné, S. "Hunting and Fishing in the Valley of Mexico in the Middle of the 16th Century." *Ethnos*, 2 (1937), pp. 56–64.

Lisanti, Luis. "Sur la nourriture des "Paulistes" entre XVIIIe et XIXe siècles." *Annales. E.S.C.* 18:3 (May–June, 1963), pp. 531–40.

Lockhart James, and Enrique Otte (eds.). *Letters and People of the Spanish Indies: The Sixteenth Century.* Cambridge: Cambridge University Press, 1976.

López de Velasco, Juan. *Geografía y descripción universal de las Indias.* Madrid: Atlas, 1971.

McCance, R. A. and E. M. Widdowson. *Breads, White and Brown: Their Place in Thought and Social History.* London: Pitman Medical Publishing Co., 1956.

MacLeod, Murdo J. "Aspects of the Internal Economy of Colonial Spanish America: Labour; Taxation; Distribution and Exchange." In Leslie Bethell (ed.). *The Cambridge History of Latin America, Colonial Latin America.* New York: Cambridge University Press, 1984, vol. 2, pp. 219–64.

————. *Spanish Central America: A Socioeconomic History, 1520–1720.* Berkeley and Los Angeles: University of California Press, 1973.

Magalhaẽs de Gandavo, Pero. *History of the Province of Santa Cruz.* Tr. John B. Stetson, Jr. New York: Cortés Society, 1922.

Malvido, Elsa. "Efectos de las epidemias y hambrunas en la población colonial de México (1519–1810)." In Enrique Florescano and Elsa Malvido (comps.). *Ensayos sobre la historia de las epidemias en México.* Mexico City: Instituto Mexicano del Seguro Social, 1982, vol. 1, pp. 179–97.

Marcus, Joyce. "The Plant World of the Sixteenth- and Seventeenth-Century Lowland Maya." In Kent V. Flannery (ed.). *Maya Subsistence: Studies in Memory of Dennis E. Puleston.* New York: Academic Press, 1982, pp. 239–73.

Masefield, G. B. "Crops and Livestock." In E. E. Rich (ed.). *Cambridge Economic*

History of Europe. Cambridge: Cambridge University Press, 1967, vol. 4, pp. 276–307.

Matesanz, José. "Introducción de la ganadería en Nueva España, 1521–1535." *Historia Mexicana*, 14:4 (April–June, 1965), pp. 533–66.

Mauro, Frédéric. *Le XVIᵉ siècle européen: Aspects économiques.* Paris: Presses Universitaires de France, 1966.

Méndez, Christóbal. *Book of Bodily Exercise.* Tr. Francisco Guerra. New Haven: Elizabeth Licht, 1960.

Millau, Francisco. *Descripción de la provincia del Río de la Plata (1772).* Buenos Aires: Espasa-Calpe, 1947.

Mintz, Sidney W. *Sweetness and Power: The Place of Sugar in Modern History.* New York: Viking, 1985.

Montemira, Marqués de. "Representación . . . que la sisa." Lima: Imprenta Real de los Niños Expósitos, 1789.

Moreno Toscano, Alejandra. "Tres problemas en la geografía del maíz, 1600–1624." *Historia Mexicana*, 14:4 (April–June, 1965), pp. 631–55.

Morgan, Edmund S. *American Slavery. American Freedom: The Ordeal of Colonial Virginia.* New York: W.W. Norton, 1975.

Morineau, Michel. "Rations de marine (Angleterre, Hollande, Suède et Russie)." *Annales. E.S.C.,* 20:6 (November–December, 1965), pp. 1150–57.

Morris, C. "Maize Beer in the Economics, Politics, and Religion of the Inca Empire" In Clifford F. Gastineau, William J. Darby, and Thomas B. Turner (eds.). *Fermented Food Beverages in Nutrition.* New York: Academic Press, 1979, pp. 21–35.

Mota y Escobar, Alonso de la. *Descripción geográfica de los reinos de Nueva Galicia, Nueva Vizcaya y Nuevo León.* Mexico City: P. Robredo, 1940.

Mote, Frederick W. "Yuan and Ming." In K. C. Chang (ed.). *Food in Chinese Culture: Anthropological and Historical Perspectives.* New Haven: Yale University Press, pp. 193–258.

Motolinía (Toribio de Benavente). *Motolinía's History of the Indians of New Spain.* Tr. Elizabeth Andros Foster. Berkeley: The Cortés Society, 1950.

Nelson, Michael. *The Development of Tropical Lands: Policy Issues in Latin America.* Baltimore and London: Johns Hopkins University Press, 1973.

Neveux, Hugues. "L'alimentation du XIVᵉ au XVIIᵉ siècle." *Revue d'Histoire Economique et Sociale,* 3 (1973), pp. 3336–79.

Newson, Linda A. "Demographic Catastrophe in Sixteenth-Century Honduras." In David J. Robinson (ed.). *Studies in Spanish American Population History.* Boulder, CO: Westview Press, 1981, pp. 217–41.

Ocaranza, Fernando. "Las grandes epidemias del siglo XVI en la Nueva España." In Enrique Florescano and Elsa Malvido (comps.). *Ensayos sobre la historia de las epidemias en México.* Mexico: Instituto Mexicano del Seguro Social, vol. 1, pp. 201–14.

Offner, Jerome. "Archival Reports of Poor Crop Yields in the Early Postconquest Texcocan Heartland and the Implications for Studies of Aztec Period Population." *American Antiquity,* 45:4 (October, 1980), pp. 848–56.

Ots Capdequi, José María. *Instituciones.* Barcelona: Salvat Editores, 1959.

Paredes, A. "Social Control of Drinking Among the Aztec Indians of Mesoamerica." *Journal of Studies on Alcohol,* 36:9 (September, 1975), pp. 1139–53.

Parry, J. H. *The Age of Reconnaissance.* New York: Mentor Books, 1964.

Paso y Troncoso, Francisco del. *Epistolario de Nueva España, 1550–1818.* 15 vols. Mexico City: José Porrua, 1939.

———. *Papeles de Nueva España: Relaciones geográficas de la Diócesis de México.* 2nd Series. Mexico City: Editorial Cosmos, 1979.

———. *Papeles de Nueva España: Relaciones geográficas de la Diócesis de Michoacán.* 2 vols. Guadalajara: Colección "Siglo XVI," 1958.

Pfefferkorn, Ignaz. *Sonora: A Description of the Province.* Tr. Theodore E. Treutlein. Albuquerque: University of New Mexico Press, 1949.

Pittman, David J., and Charles R. Snyder (eds.). *Society, Culture and Drinking Patterns.* New York: John Wiley and Sons, 1962.

Poitrineau, A. "L'alimentation populaire en Auvergne au XVIIIe siècle." *Annales. E.S.C.,* 17:2 (March–April, 1962), pp. 323–31.

Prado Júnior, Caio. *The Colonial Background of Modern Brazil.* Tr. Suzette Macedo. Berkeley and Los Angeles: University of California Press, 1969.

Puiz, Anne-Maria. "Alimentation populaire et sous-alimentation au XVIIe siècle. Le cas de Genève et de sa région." In Jean-Jacque Hémardinquer (ed.). *Pour une histoire de l'alimentation* (Paris: Cahiers de Annales, 1970), pp. 129–45.

Puleston, Dennis E. "The Role of Ramón in Maya Subsistence." In Kent V. Flannery (ed.). *Maya Subsistence: Studies in Memory of Dennis E. Puleston.* New York: Academic Press, 1982, pp. 353–66.

Quintín Olascoaga, José. *Bromatología de los alimentos industrializados.* Mexico City: n.p., 1963.

Recopilación de leyes de los Reynos de las Indias. 3 vols. Madrid: Gráficas Ultra, 1943.

Roca, Juan, and Roberto Llamas. "Consideraciones sobre el valor alimenticio del pulque." *Anales del Instituto de Biología,* 10:1–2 (March–June, 1939), pp. 364–71.

Rodrigues, José Honório. *Brazil and Africa.* Tr. Richard A. Mazzara and Sam Hileman. Berkeley and Los Angeles: University of California Press, 1965.

Rotberg, Robert I., and Theodore K. Rabb (eds.). *Hunger and History: The Impact of Changing Food Production and Consumption Patterns on Society.* Cambridge: Cambridge University Press, 1985.

Rouse, John E. *The Criollo: Spanish Cattle in the Americas.* Norman: University of Oklahoma Press, 1977.

Rowe, John Howland. "Inca Culture at the Time of the Spanish Conquest." In Julian H. Steward (ed.). *Handbook of South American Indians: The Andean Civilizations.* Washington, D.C.: Smithsonian Institution, 1946, vol. 2, pp. 183–330.

Ruvalcaba Mercado, Jesús. "Agricultura colonial temprana y transformación social en Tepeapulco y Tulancingo (1521–1610). *Historia Mexicana,* 33:4 (April–June, 1984), pp. 424–44.

Sahagún, Bernardino de. *Historia general de las cosas de Nueva España.* 5 vols. Mexico City: Editorial Pedro Robredo, 1938.

Salaman, Redcliffe N. *The History and Social Influence of the Potato.* Cambridge: University Press, 1969.

Salinas Meza, René. "Raciones alimenticias en Chile colonial." *Historia* (Santiago), 12 (1974–1975), pp. 57–76.

Sánchez-Albornoz, Nicolas. *The Population of Latin America.* Tr. W.A.R. Richardson. Berkeley and Los Angeles: University of California Press, 1974.

Sanders, William T., and Barbara J. Price. *Mesoamerica: The Evolution of a Civilization.* New York: Random House, 1968.

Santos Vilhena, Luís dos. *A Bahia no século XVIII.* Bahia: Editôra Itapua, 1969.

Sauer, Carl Ortwin. *The Early Spanish Main.* Berkeley and Los Angeles: University of California Press, 1966.

Scardaville, Michael C. "Crime and the Urban Poor: Mexico City in the Late Colonial Period." Ph.D. dissertation. University of Florida, 1977.

Schwartz, Stuart B. "Colonial Brazil, c. 1580–c. 1750: Plantations and Peripheries." In Leslie Bethell (ed.). *The Cambridge History of Latin America. Colonial Latin America.* Cambridge: Cambridge University Press, vol. 2., pp. 423–500.

Scrimshaw, N. S., and J. E. Gordon (eds.). *Malnutrition, Learning, and Behavior.* Cambridge, MA: MIT Press, 1968.

Silva Santisteban, Carlos Malpica. *Crónica del hambre en el Perú.* Lima: Moncloa Compodónico Ediciones, 1970.

Simpson, Lesley Byrd. *Exploitation of Land in Central Mexico in the Sixteenth Century.* Ibero-Americana, 36. Berkeley and Los Angeles: University of California Press, 1952.

Slicher van Bath, B. H. *The Agrarian History of Western Europe, A.D. 500–1850.* Tr. Olive Ordish. London: Edward Arnold, 1963.

Solano, Francisco de. "An Introduction to the Study of Provisioning in the Colonial City." In Richard P. Schaedel, Jorge E. Hardoy, and Nora Scott Kinzer (eds.). *Urbanization in the Americas From Its Beginnings to the Present.* The Hague: Mouton Publishers, 1978, pp. 99–129.

Solórzano y Pereyra, Juan de. *Política Indiana.* 5 vols. Madrid: Compañía Ibero-Americana, 1930.

Sorokin, Pitirim A. *Hunger as a Factor in Human Affairs.* Tr. Elena P. Sorokin. Gainesville: University Presses of Florida, 1975.

Sorre, Maximilien. *Les fondements biologiques de la géographie humaine: essai d'une écologie de l'homme.* Paris: A. Colins, 1971.

Spalding, Karen. *Huarochiri: An Andean Society Under Inca and Spanish Rule.* Palo Alto: Stanford University Press, 1984.

Stern, Steve J. *Peru's Indian Peoples and the Challenge of Spanish Conquest.* Madison: University of Wisconsin Press, 1982.

Stouff, Louis. *Ravitaillement et alimentation en Provence aux 14e et 15e siècles.* Paris: Mouton, 1970.

Super, John C. "Bread and the Provisioning of Mexico City in the Late Eighteenth Century." *Jahrbuch für Geschichte von Staat, Wirtschaft und Gesellschaft Lateinamerikas,* 19 (1982), pp. 159–82.

———. "The Formation of Nutritional Regimes in Colonial Latin America." In

John C. Super and Thomas Wright (eds.). *Food, Politics, and Society in Latin America*. Lincoln: University of Nebraska Press, 1985, pp. 1–23.

————. "Pan, alimentación y política en Querétaro en la última decada del siglo XVIII." *Historia Mexicana*, 30:2 (October–December, 1980), pp. 247–72.

————. "Sources and Methods for the Study of Historical Nutrition in Latin America." *Historical Methods*. 14:1 (Winter, 1981), pp. 22–30.

————. "Spanish Diet in the Atlantic Crossing, the 1570s." *Terrae Incognitae*, 16 (1984), pp. 57–70.

————. *La vida en Querétaro durante la colonia 1531–1810*. Mexico City: Fondo de Cultura Económica, 1983.

Swann, Michael M. "The Demographic Impact of Disease and Famine in Late Colonial Northern Mexico." *Geoscience and Man*, 21 (1980), pp. 97–109.

Taylor, William B. *Drinking, Homicide, and Rebellion in Colonial Mexican Villages*. Stanford: Stanford University Press, 1979.

Torquemada, Juan de. *Monarquía Indiana*. 3 vols. Mexico City: Editorial Salvador Chávez Hayhoe, 1943.

Trapham, Thomas. *A Discourse of the State of Health in the Island of Jamaica . . .* London: R. Boulter, 1679.

Tryon, Thomas. *Friendly Advice to the Gentlemen-Planters of the East and West Indies*. London: Andrew Soule, 1684.

Unanue, José Hipólito. *Observaciones sobre el clima de Lima . . .* Lima: Imp. Lux, 1940.

Urteaga, Horacio H. (ed.). *Fundación española del Cusco y ordenanzas para su gobierno*. Lima: Talleres Gráficas Sanmarti y Cia, 1926.

Van Young, Eric. *Hacienda and Market in Eighteenth-Century Mexico: The Rural Economy of the Guadalajara Region, 1675–1820*. Berkeley and Los Angeles: University of California Press, 1981.

Vásquez de Warman, Irene. "El pósito y la ahóndiga en la Nueva España." *Historia Mexicana*, 17:3 (January–March, 1968), pp. 395–426.

Vázquez, Mario C. "La chicha en los paises andinos," *América Indígena*, 27 (1967), pp. 265–282.

Vázquez de Espinosa, Antonio. *Compendium and Description of the West Indies*. Tr. Charles Upson Clark. Washington, D.C.: Smithsonian Institution, 1942.

————. *Descripción de la Nueva España en el siglo XVII*. Mexico City: Editorial Pastria, 1944.

Vicens Vives, Jaime. *An Economic History of Spain*. Tr. Frances M. López-Morillas. Princeton: Princeton University Press, 1969.

————. *Historia social y económica de España y América*. 5 vols. Barcelona: Editorial Teide, 1957.

Viesca T., Carlos. "Hambruna y epidemia en Anáhuac (1450–1454) en la época de Moctezuma Ilhuicamina." In Enrique Florescano and Elsa Malvido (comps.). *Ensayos sobre la historia de las epidemias en México*. Mexico City: Instituto Mexicano del Seguro Social, 1982. vol. 2, pp. 157–68.

Wachtel, Nathan. "The Indian and the Spanish Conquest." In Leslie Bethell (ed.). *The Cambridge History of Latin America. Colonial Latin America*. Cambridge: Cambridge University Press, 1984, vol. 1, pp. 207–248.

Wallerstein, Immanuel. *The Modern World-System: Capitalist Agriculture and the*

Origins of the European World-Economy in the Sixteenth Century. New York: Academic Press, 1974.

Watkins, Susan Cotts, and Etienne van de Walle. "Nutrition, Mortality, and Population Size: Malthus' Court of Last Resort." In Robert I. Rotberg and Theordore K. Rabb (eds.). *Hunger and History: The Impact of Changing Food Production and Consumption Patterns on Society*. Cambridge: Cambridge University Press, 1985, pp. 7–28.

West, Robert C., and John P. Augelli. *Middle America: Its Lands and Peoples*. Englewood Cliffs, NJ: Prentice-Hall, 1966.

Wyczanski, A. "The Social Structure of Nutrition, a Case." *Acta Poloniae historica*, 18 (1968), pp. 63–74.

Zorita, Alonso de. *Life and Labor in Ancient Mexico*. Tr. Benjamin Keen. New Brunswick, NJ: Rutgers University Press, 1963.

Index

abasto de carne, 47, 49, 50, 83
Africa, 15, 53
agriculture, 8, 14–22, 42, 66, 67; crop
  yields, 20–23; farmer/rancher conflict, 42, 55, 56; grain/cattle conflict,
  30–32, 37, 38; impact of European,
  19, 55–58
Aguirre Beltrán, Gonzalo, 4
alcohol, theories of, 75–77
alhóndiga, 47–50, 59, 83, 86
Alvarez Ossorio y Redín, Miguel, 33
America, comparisons within, 3, 16
Andes region, 14–17, 62, 72, 77; crops,
  20, 21, 34–37, 57, 66–68; economic
  crisis, 86–88; exports, 19; livestock,
  27, 56. *See also* Peru
animal foods, 14, 26–32, 68, 69, 84, 85,
  97 n 24

Argentina, 28, 31
Atlantic trade, 15, 30, 93 n 12
atole, 33
Aztecs, the, 17, 62, 66, 68, 74, 75

Bajío, the, 18, 28, 37
Bakewell, Peter, 86, 87
bananas, 15, 23
Barbados, 58
beef, 6, 28, 29
beverages, 72
Book of Bodily Exercises (Méndez), 71
Book of Spiritual Governance
  (Ovando), 40
Borah, Woodrow, and Sherburne F.
  Cook, 4, 6, 52, 53, 61, 70, 72, 86
Boxer, Charles, 10
Brading, David, 22

129